Mysticism
for
Modern Times

Mysticism
for
Modern Times

Conversations with
Willigis Jäger

Edited by Christoph Quarch, PhD
Translated by Paul Shepherd

Liguori/Triumph
LIGUORI, MISSOURI

Published by Liguori/Triumph
An imprint of Liguori Publications
Liguori, Missouri
www.liguori.org

Translation copyright 2006 by Liguori Publications

Previously published under the title *Die Welle ist das Meer*, copyright 2000, by Verlag Herder Freiburg im Breisgau, Germany.

All rights reserved. No part of this publication may be reproduced, stored in a retrieval system, or transmitted in any form or by any means—electronic, mechanical, photocopy, recording, or any other—except for brief quotations in printed reviews, without the prior permission of the publisher.

Library of Congress Cataloging-in-Publication Data

Jäger, Willigis.
    [Die Welle ist das Meer. English.]
    Mysticism for modern times : conversations with Willigis Jäger / translated by Paul Shepherd, edited by Christoph Quarch, PhD.—1st U.S. ed.
        p. cm.
    ISBN 0-7648-1285-8
    1. Mysticism. 2. Jäger, Willigis—Interviews. 3. Catholic Church—Germany—Clergy—Interviews. I. Quarch, Christoph. II. Title.
    BV5082.3.J3513 2006
    248.2'2—dc22   2005035942

Scripture references are taken from the *New Revised Standard Version Bible*, copyright 1989 by the Division of Christian Education of the National Council of Churches of Christ in the U.S.A. Used by permission. All rights reserved.

Excerpts from pages 9, 127, 181, and 226 are from *Meister Eckhart: A Modern Translation* by Raymond Bernard Blakney, copyright 1941 by Harper and Brothers. Reprinted by permission of HarperCollins Publishers.

Excerpt from *Ecce Homo* by Friedrich Nietzsche, translated by R. J. Hollingdale, copyright 1992, used with permission of Penguin Putnam, Inc.

Excerpts from *Collected Works of C. G. Jung, Volume 11: Psychology and Religion: West and East*, copyright 1970, edited and translated by Gerhard Adler and R.F.C. Hull. Used with permission of Princeton University Press.

Printed in the United States of America
10 09 08 07 06   5 4 3 2 1
First U.S. Edition 2006

Contents

PART TWO
THE SPIRITUAL PRACTICE OF MYSTICISM

Preface

IT IS A TWO-HOUR TRAIN RIDE from Würzburg to Stuttgart, and two hours was the length of the lively discussion I had with Michael Strauss, my colleague at that time, in a train compartment on a January evening in 1999. We were on our way back from an interview with Willigis Jäger, which was to appear a short time later in the Protestant journal *Evangelische Kommentare*. We were still in an inspired frame of mind, but it was of an intensity we had never experienced before on our many trips together to interview people for the magazine. The matters we had discussed would influence further discussions between Michael and myself for many days. For me, at least, it was as if the door had opened to a spiritual world whose existence I had somehow already known about, but which had never lain so clear and open before me as during that interview.

Willigis Jäger spoke about mysteries of religion and of faith without wandering off into mystification or fancifulness. On the contrary, here was a man who understood how to speak about life and death, about resurrection and rebirth, about miracles and the sacraments, in a way that did justice to the intellectual demands I had acquired during years of studies in philosophy. Here was a man who spoke about God without falling back on the worn-out concepts and phrases that have spoiled many a Sunday church service for me. And yet he spoke in such a way that I could recognize again the faith of my childhood in much that he said—not so naive as

before, but newly rendered in the light of an interpretation that was
doubtless the fruit of a deep spiritual experience. In short, I had the
feeling that there might be, in the end, a faith—a *Christian* faith—
that could stand up to my own rigorous criteria of intellectual honesty while answering my longing for authentic religiosity.
    But would it also agree with the criteria of Christian dogma and
doctrine? Michael Strauss was not so sure. And precisely that con-
troversy was no small factor behind the continuous fruitfulness of
our discussions. It was clear to me that much of what Willigis Jäger
says and thinks would be hard to digest for people coming from a
traditional Christian background. Like my colleague, I found it a source
of dissatisfaction that Willigis Jäger's insights were fed by sources of
experience that were not accessible to us, or at least have yet to become so. But the unconditional honesty and authority with which
our dialogue partner developed his ideas left no doubt that it would
be well worth our while to occupy ourselves more intensively with
the wisdom of this man. Thus evolved the idea of following up the
magazine interview with a book-length interview.
    Willigis Jäger agreed to the idea—somewhat hesitant at first, but
finally convinced that a book of this sort could be helpful in making
his experiences and knowledge accessible to people lacking the time
and leisure to read one of his more detailed expositions. We met with
Willigis Jäger on two weekends in Haus St. Benedikt in Würzburg.
Once again, I encountered an extremely attentive and concentrated
discussion partner who, although sometimes groping for the right
word, never attempted to evade a question.

CHRISTOPH QUARCH
FULDA, AUGUST 2000

Foreword

DURING MANY YEARS of living in Japan I gained insight into the Eastern worldview while having the opportunity to observe the structure of Christian faith from the outside. I realized that religions are models that we use to understand the world and ourselves. While models spring from experience, they do not always portray reality. In many cases they are based on postulates that, over time, are simply repeated without question. Even the empirical field of science explains complicated life processes with an awareness that models—postulates, theories, laws—are not life itself, but simply an explanation of it. As such, scientific models change as life changes.

Similarly, religions also provide models for understanding complicated life processes, particularly with respect to God and creation. Unfortunately, however, religions do not always adapt to fluctuations in human understanding or growth. If our view of the world or God changes, then the religions should have the courage to create new models or to interpret the old ones in new ways. Otherwise, like any stale theory or law, they may act more to block the way than to open it.

This book was written for those people who wish to rediscover God in light of various ancient and emerging perspectives of God. It provides access to Eastern religious traditions in order to develop the fullness of the Western mystical tradition. Overall, its thesis can be expressed as follows: We should not limit ourselves to understanding God as the creator of an ontologically different world. Rather we should

realize the fullness of God as the unity of being *and* nonbeing, where
there is no separation between God and the world, between spirit
and matter, between being and nonbeing. The concept of "God" will
be examined here as a single reality that reveals itself on many levels—being and nonbeing—but retains a distinct identity. It is like
the ocean that reveals itself through a myriad of unique waves; it has
many dimensions, but it is comprised of one body of water.

I am aware that some of the ideas in this book will incite fear in
many people, perhaps causing them to take a stand against them.
For that very reason, they could lead to a dialogue about religion and
mysticism. Nothing in this book is propagated as the absolute truth.
I am not trying to coerce anyone into a supreme system of interpretation. Nor am I attempting to devalue existing religious ideas or
institutions. I am simply trying to see old truths in a different light,
which does not mean degrading other views. It is my hope that the
book can provide insights into the meaning of our human existence.
My extensive experience in pastoral work tells me that many people
are searching for answers, and that they will be encouraged by reading these thoughts to continue their spiritual journey.

Since my childhood I have been searching for an answer to the
basic question: What is the meaning of my life on this totally insig-
nificant grain of dust at the edge of an incredibly vast universe? Through
Eastern religious traditions, I have found a depth of spirituality that
heightens my Western Christian mysticism, one which begins to un-
fold the ultimate questions of life.

Whether by chance or through an act of providence, I am for-
mulating this dialogue in Bursfelde, a former Benedictine abbey where
I am presently leading a meditation course. It was in this very monastery that a reform movement had its beginnings in the Middle Ages,
when, under the influence of contemplative mysticism, a new form
of religiosity developed among the laity—the so-called *devotio moderna*.
Originally practiced in lay circles, it eventually found its way into
the monasteries, particularly in Bursfelde where a period of private

meditation was added to the celebration of the liturgy and the recitation of the Divine Office. Today, it is once again primarily members of the laity who come together in various groups to practice this form of contemplative prayer. I offer these conversations to encourage all people to courageously embrace their spiritual journeys.

WILLIGIS JÄGER

Introduction

On the Cusp of a Millennium of the Spirit: Awakening the Need for Mysticism

AS THE DIRECTOR of Haus St. Benedikt, a center of spirituality in Würzburg, Germany, you deal with guests and students who are searching for something in their own way. What motivates them to embark on a spiritual path?

Many of the women and men who come to our center no longer feel at home in their Christian milieu. They are no longer able to derive much, if anything, from the faith of traditional Christian churches. Religion, as such, neither helps them in dealing with everyday life nor does it agree with their worldview. How could it? Unfortunately, many churches fall well short of defining faith with respect to contemporary reality. After all, many of the most sacred dogmas were formulated when the earth was still considered to be flat and the stars were holes in the firmament.

Findings in astrophysics have shown us that humanity is not the center of the universe. Our earth is a grain of dust, one speck in a relatively small galaxy that itself is among nearly 125 billion other galaxies, at last count. This universe of ours, which perhaps began with a so-called "big bang" billions of years ago, has been expanding ever since at a speed close to that of light. We now know about pulsating quasars and black holes. Such theories provide the lens through which we interpret the modern world. We take them for granted, even incorporating them into our understanding of daily life.

People are searching to rearticulate religious experience, to rediscover ancient spirituality in an accessible, understandable, realistic way. This is not a rejection of institutional religion, but a movement to awaken its fundamental insight within a modern worldview.

Why do people persist in believing in something that disagrees with their own knowledge?

People need religious ideas that can give them meaning and hope, neither of which is expendable. A characteristic of our species is the ability to think about ourselves, which necessarily entails thinking about the meaning of life, about suffering, death, and an afterlife. According to C. G. Jung (1875–1961), belief trumps knowledge in order to avert despair even if expressing a worldview that might not have caused any serious problems for people in medieval times, but which has become incomprehensible for people of today and no longer do justice to the last five centuries of the development of the spirit. The old paradigm no longer supports reality, and people despair from not knowing why they really live.

Is this what draws them to you?

Yes, although it is not the only reason. Even believing and practicing Christians come to me. They either have doubts about their faith, or they wish to broaden their understanding of spirituality. Many have become aware that the faith of their childhood no longer has the power to carry them through life, let alone through death. A large number of visitors do not belong to any church or confession, but they are deeply religious in their own way. While spirituality has played no role in their lives up to now, they come with awareness that it is absolutely necessary to unravel the mystery of their lives.

What is the reason for this heightened awareness of spirituality?

There is no easy explanation, although we can cite a number of possible reasons. For a while now I've noticed a phenomenon of satiety in our society. People in the West are so blessed with material plenty that they eventually lose sight of their place in creation. They find it hard to orient themselves amid all the ideologies that flood our lives at dizzying speed from all corners of the globe via technology and the media. Politicians—the so-called voice of the people— either don't know the truth or they avoid telling it, believing that such information will be too depressing and not particularly helpful for elections. We are manipulated by advertising and selective news coverage. All of this results in deep-seated unrest among many people today. But it also forces them to search for a system of values that can act as a basis for our future coexistence on this planet.

During the past several centuries, European humanism emerged as the universal system of values for the Western world. Recently, however, humanism has fallen into discredit. Are people searching for a new ethic?

A while back the German philosopher Peter Sloterdijk (born 1947) wrote a scathing critique of humanism in which he accused it of having failed to transform humans into beings who are in agreement with their own ethical demands. Sloterdijk called for the creation of new rules for the "human park" of the future. Lying behind his insight is the question, filled with foreboding, of where our species (*homo sapiens*) is headed, given our obvious immaturity. Neither mainstream religiosity, Marxism, existentialism, nor capitalism have been successful in turning us into better creatures. Nor has humanism—whether in its ancient form, its Christian form, or the form of the Enlightenment—made a significant contribution to the further development of what it means to be human. Indeed, the opposite would seem true, particularly when we turn our attention to the events of the twentieth century. In the wake of Stalin, Hitler, Mao and Pol Pot, in the face of ethnic conflicts in Africa, crushing poverty in Latin America, war in the Middle East, and growing crime rates around the world, we can no longer avoid the question of what actually makes us human.

In the face of the tragic failure of humanism in the twentieth century, we must rephrase the question of what is necessary for the education of the human race. Sloterdijk is certainly right in this respect.
Nietzsche (whom Sloterdijk quotes) already saw this more than a
century ago. In *Thus Spoke Zarathustra,* he compared youth (and we
can extend this to include our entire life) to a camel that patiently
kneels and allows itself to be loaded with goods. It then staggers to
its feet and carries its burden through the desert, where it turns into
a lion. The more the camel has carried, the stronger the lion. But
now the lion has to kill a dragon, a dragon whose name is "Thou
Shalt!" When the dragon is killed, the lion turns into a child, who then
develops an identity based on his deepest essence. With these metaphors, Nietzsche satirizes those who supposedly possess a monopoly
on education. Far from advocating an overthrow of education altogether, Nietzsche's metaphor makes a desperate announcement that
we have been unable to educate people to be people. He is aware of
an immense lack in the education of the human race through religion, theology, and philosophy, not to mention social and political
systems. This lack brings us to the question of the meaning of education in a broader sense. Are there possibilities of socialization that
can ensure a life for us all worthy of our dignity as human beings?

*Sloterdijk says that we can no longer simply leave the answers to the
philosophers and theologians since, sooner or later, the question will
become a topic of discussion for genetic technicians and biochemists.
His maxim is thus "anthropo-technology" instead of humanistic education. What do you think of such ideas?*

Words like anthropo-technology, prenatal selection, and genetic
manipulation fill us with apprehension. And such fears are justified,
since no one really knows what the human race will be like in the
future. Sloterdijk is right, though, when he says that "taming the human
species" can evidently no longer occur by resorting to moral commandments and prohibitions. We need more than rules to forge our
future life together on this planet. But it would also be wrong to assume that we can achieve our true form through selective breeding.

Our powers of reasoning have been corrupted by a life-threatening egocentrism. We find ourselves now at a dead end to which a "hypertrophy of the rational" combined with a destructive narcissism has taken us. Given this fact, I see only one solution: True humanism can never be achieved by commandments, but only through a mystical experience of our unity with all of existence. We have to reach our actual source, our true existence, our divine center, or whatever you want to call it. Any moral system imposed from outside is doomed to failure in the long run. Therefore, we must try to inform our children about how they can live in a sensible manner in our society. We need rules, all the way from the red light on the street corner to responsibilities in society. But rules are not enough. A true transformation of the human being can only come from the depths of our being.

How can people be motivated to desire such a transformation from the depths of their being?

It's not as difficult as it seems. All of us have retained a sense or an inkling of a place where all our questions are answered, and an increasing number of people are searching for that place. When these people come to me, I guide them on a spiritual path that leads to an experience of what is spoken of in the sacred books of different religions, what is celebrated in rituals and the sacraments, and what the churches originally promised. Briefly put, it is a path leading to an experience of what religions have as their goal: God, divinity, emptiness, Brahman. I find that these words are expressions of final things and of unity.

You imply that religions have failed to deliver something that they "origi-
nally promised." Does that mean they are no longer able to communicate
religious experience? Is it, in the final analysis, the need for religious or
spiritual experience that brings people to you?

Yes and no. Among those people who come to us, there are those
who desire such an experience and those who have already had one.
Common to both groups is a knowledge or sense that conveying or
imparting religious faith in purely intellectual terms is no longer satisfactory. They already know they can never find the answer to their
questions about the meaning of life along a purely cognitive path.

Is that the reason why many churches continue to decline in attendance?

One of the main problems of the modern churches is their failure to communicate the great treasure of their mystical and spiritual
traditions. The mystical elements of Christianity, once so prevalent,
are barely present in contemporary Western forms of religion. Note
how, for example, the great scientists of the twentieth century (Heisenberg, Pauly, Schroedinger) turned more to Hinduism or Buddhism
than to Christianity in their search for a language to express the spiritual dimension of their discoveries in physics. How many people
today are even aware that the Christian mystical tradition possesses
a wisdom and depth that is equally potent as the teachings of the
East? Christian mystics, such as Meister Eckhart, Johannes Tauler,
and Nicholas of Cusa, have fallen into oblivion.

Is this because predominant expressions of Christian theology have
glossed over this mystical treasure?

Mystical experience has been reduced to a fringe existence in recent theology and catechesis. For example, the nine-hundred-page
Catechism of the Catholic Church makes no explicit mention of mysticism. In modern Catholic teaching, it is classified as a subdivision
of dogmatic theology. Analyzed alongside the rational teachings about
faith, it can only find expression through abstract rationalism. This
has been a source of considerable difficulty for Catholic mystics. If

they want to communicate their experiences, they have to do so through the filter of dogmatic theology. As such, mysticism loses its immediacy and uniqueness. Mystical streams of Hinduism and Buddhism, and to a certain extent Islam, enjoy a much wider sphere of influence because they developed much more freely than Christian mysticism.

Is it simply the dominance of dogmatic theology that clips the wings of mysticism in Catholicism, or is it its theological method in general?

That's a difficult question. The fact is that there has been no place for mysticism in Christian theology for the past two hundred years. Theologians that seek a rationalization of faith are not interested in mysticism with its "irrational" reputation. Instead, they advocate secular scientific methods for investigating theology. Such inquiry, I believe, is the result of a fundamental misunderstanding of revelation. Teachers of wisdom in all religions agree that the core of human faith can only be found in a dimension beyond all conceptual expression or rational understanding.

How was such a rationalistic misunderstanding possible in Christianity?

It started a long time ago, perhaps originating in Aristotelian philosophy. In the theology based on that philosophical tradition, God is ruler *above* all things: the pinnacle *of* creation, but not *in* creation. God is the end goal to which all things strive, but God does not flow within creation. In other words, the Aristotelian God is not an overflowing fullness revealing itself as creation. Writing under the influence of this Aristotelian philosophy, Albert the Great and Thomas Aquinas had a major influence on the Christian theology of the Middle Ages. They reinforced the idea of a God *outside* the world, determining its fate like the Yahweh of ancient Israel. But that's not all; since God was objectified, they opened the door for scientific analysis of revelation in subsequent centuries. This, in turn, led to an insufficient understanding of mysticism.

What consequences has this theistic approach had for Christian theology?

Theism—a philosophical system that accepts a transcendent and personal God—can lead to a dualistic view of the world, resulting in a wide gap between God and creation. The world and God emerge as ontologically different realities. According to Christian theism, we are in a "valley of tears," striving to escape to a transcendent realm via the saving bridge of the cross. The fact that Jesus is understood by Christians as the savior of humanity is a consequence of theistic thinking. Modern soteriology (theology of salvation), Christology (theological interpretation of Christ), and the theology of sacrifice have meaning only within a theistic perspective.

Are you saying that Jesus himself never claimed to be a savior, and that this description is only a theistic interpretation of what he did?

I'm not denying that Jesus sometimes preferred a theistic interpretation of his life and teachings. We can understand this from the nature of the language of his time. What's decisive here, however, is how Christianity placed an incredible burden upon itself by propagating a theology of salvation that did not actually originate with Jesus—it was Saint Paul who introduced it. This is so in two ways: First, because it is hardly possible today to make any educated person believe that someone died on the cross two thousand years ago to atone for our sins. Second, because a disdain of the world resulted in a disdain of all earthly things—the earth, nature, women, the body, sexuality and the senses—a view that is no longer tenable. I'm aware, of course, that such statements fail to do justice to the complexity of the subject. Nevertheless, it seems to me that there is truth to them with respect to two thousand years of Christianity.

But such dualism is certainly not found in Christianity alone.

That's true. We find theistic and dualistic elements not only in Christianity, Islam, and Judaism but also in Buddhism and Hinduism as they are practiced today, to the extent that they are religions and are not following the mystical paths of their founders. The Buddhist belief in *Amida*, for example, hardly differs from its counterpart in Christianity. On a visit to India, I saw animal sacrifices meant to appease the god Kali. As is true in other religions, a division is imposed between God and the world, after which a surmounting of that division, in addition to salvation at a later date, is promised as a result of renunciation and sacrifices. It is precisely in this achievement of surmounting the division that their promise of salvation is found.

If all the major religions contain dualistic elements, one is tempted to suspect that theistic explanations of God—as an subjectification of God—are to be found in the nature of the human intellect. Is a non-theistic theology even imaginable? Or, to reframe the question, isn't theism the only possible way to speak about God?

That would be going too far. Reviewing the history of philosophy, we see that not all of the major thinkers supported a dualistic-theistic approach. Curiously, it was none other than Aristotle's teacher, Plato, who played a definitive role in the West in creating a non-theistic theology. Plato, in contrast to Aristotle, does not recognize an ontological dualism, despite all the false interpretations of his writings. But his philosophy survived only as an undercurrent in European thinking, or in mysticism, to be more accurate. The third-century thinkers Proclus and Plotinus were Neoplatonists, as were Evagrius of Pontus in the fourth century and Dionysius the Aeropagite in the fifth. Meister Eckhart, Nicholas of Cusa, and Gottfried Leibniz all trace their roots back to Plato.

Could you explain how?

In Platonic philosophy God is both *in* the world and *outside* the world. Matter alone does not exist; it only becomes reality through the timeless ideas manifested in it. It is interesting to note that this "idealism" now enjoys a new interest among modern scientists. Quantum mechanics is an indication that we are moving toward a worldview similar to the Platonic view in many respects. I am well aware that we can argue whether Plato can actually be understood in this way. Nevertheless, the fact that mystics refer back to him gives an added edge to this interpretation.

What are the most important areas of concurrence between Platonic philosophy and mysticism?

We find the most important concurrence in the realization that there is no dividing gap between God and the world, that the world is no less than the revelation of the divine and, accordingly, that salvation can be understood not as a bridging of a gap but as an awakening to our actual essence. In that sense, it has always been the actual goal of all religious thinkers and founders of religions to free people from their benighted state and lead them to an experience of the divine. They understood salvation to be a realization. Here is where I find the essential significance of Jesus: Not in his death of atonement on the cross for sinful humanity, but in showing us a way to an experience of unity with the original divine principle. It was an experience that he had had himself and which enabled him not only to refer to God in an intimate way as "Father" but also to say: "The Father and I are one" (John 10:30) or "And whoever sees me sees him who sent me" (John 12:45) or "…before Abraham was, I am" (John 8:58). It would thus be a perfectly legitimate understanding of ourselves as Christians to embark on a path of realization in a mystical consciousness in imitation of Christ.

Despite a growing awareness of spirituality and mysticism in the churches, people searching for religious experience rarely knock on the doors of the church. They look for salvation outside established institutions.

Under the influence of Buddhist and Hindu traditions, small groups and communities have developed in the Western world having little or nothing to do with the churches. It would appear that mysticism has "emigrated" from the churches. Of course, some of this is pseudo-mysticism and many a charlatan is profiting well from selling "meaning and fulfillment." The broad-based New Age movement has also given rise to many questionable tendencies. At the same time, we must also admit that those driven in that direction are often seriously seeking for the truth and have evidently found nothing to their satisfaction elsewhere.

You said that many people have already had an identity crisis by the time they come to you. Do you have the feeling that such identity crises are on the increase?

Yes, and it's also my impression that the reason can be found in the lifestyles of our society. Traditional patterns of marriage and the family are disintegrating to some extent as regional and national differences disappear. At the same time, we're experiencing an extreme acceleration of all life processes. People are burned out and dissatisfied. Among my other activities, I direct a group known as the Forum for Management and Spirituality. There I repeatedly hear the complaint that people fail to find any real sense of fulfillment in their lives despite business success. Many of their colleagues have already dropped out of the race, often as the result of a heart attack or mental breakdown. Characteristic of these developments is the feeling that something is lacking in their lives, particularly in the higher echelons of an enterprise. For many people this can often result in physical illness, as we see in the dramatic increase in chronic ailments. When so many people no longer see any meaning in their lives, the situation has elements of a crisis. But we shouldn't just lament the situation. Crises are also something positive, or can be, at least, if we recognize them as such and use them to make a new start. Unfortunately that only happens in the minority of cases.

Why?

Because people are alone in their crises. One of the central problems of modern life is loneliness and isolation. And the situation isn't helped in the least by the fact that we can now communicate with everyone in the world via the Internet. It's a bitter irony when a marriage falls apart because the husband, for example, is only interested in virtual communication in a chat room and forgets his wife in the process. We won't find anything we truly need on the Internet. No genuine encounters happen there, and genuine encounters are the only ones that can relieve us of our loneliness and isolation.

Can such widespread lack of orientation also have something to do with the fact that what you describe does not offer a sense of belonging and identity to those in crisis situations: a feeling of belonging and identity? Studies have shown that "security" is what the majority of Christians expect from the church. Those who turn away from organized religion often end up in sects or "psycho-groups" that promise security and a feeling of belonging.

The spiritually homeless—and that's an incredibly large number of people today—have the choice of accepting their homelessness and using it as an opportunity to search for their true home or identity, or attempting to find an *ersatz* home in groups or organizations that promise security and salvation. On the mental level of that movement emerges fundamentalism, which is basically nothing more than a desperate search for a true home by people who have lost their orientation in life. Fundamentalism promises believers salvation according to the motto: "When you do this and this, and conform faithfully and piously to the rules of the community, you will go to heaven." Many fundamentalist sects have had considerable success with this strategy, although the people who join them have been helped precious little.

*But don't we find such pat promises of salvation in the organized church-
es as well?*

Of course, and not only in the Christian churches. You find such
simplified logic even in Hinduism or Buddhism or Islam: "Obey the
commandments on earth and you will be saved when you die, or at
least be reborn in a better existence." This is the basic structure of
what we could call the *exoteric* form of religion. But here we must
distinguish it from its *esoteric* core—the mystical dimension—which
in most cases is not as easy to recognize.

*But it is precisely this conventional, exoteric religiosity that many peo-
ple are turning away from, at least in Western society. How is it, then,
that many of these people nevertheless end up in dogmatic or fundamentalist forms of belief?*

We have to make a distinction here. There are naive and simple
forms of religiosity where the faithful ask their god for aid and trouble
themselves very little with theological or existential questions. The
Western world, with the triumphal inroads of the modern, scientific
worldview, has lost this "conventional" dimension of belief. This has
resulted in a crisis in orientation that in turn has produced a retreat
back to fundamentalism and sectarianism just described. But it is no
longer the original, naive piety. That has been irreversibly lost.

*Should the Christian churches endeavor to correct their picture of the
world and humanity? After all, there is a strong tendency, especially in
Roman Catholicism, to refuse to curry favor with the spirit of the times.*

The question here is not one of currying favor with the spirit of
the times, but whether we are prepared to take seriously the findings
of modern science as questions for theology. We must, at least, take
those findings seriously enough that we will be prepared, when necessary, to put old, untenable doctrines to rest or at least give them a
new interpretation. But that's only the first step. An additional problem of the churches is that their image of God is based on an already
obsolete worldview. If they want to reach modern people already

influenced by developments in science without going through intellectual contortions, they will have to reconsider what they're offering the masses in the area of theology. Up to now, however, they haven't had the courage to depart from the structure of faith in conformity with the system and to make fresh attempts at reinterpretation. I wish for more courageous theologians.

Do you mean theologians with an understanding of mysticism and spirituality?

I mean theologians who won't, like the majority of their colleagues, remain satisfied with an intellectualistic view of God. The fact that most theologians bar the way to mysticism is only one of the results of such a myopic theology. The other result, which is no less serious, is that theologians ignore the bodily dimension of life. Religiosity is not limited to the intellect. Religious experiences can also occur through the body or psyche. Indeed, many people are having such experiences today through those channels. Just think of the present "wellness" mode or the tremendous interest in sports. Whether it is in-line skating, hang-gliding, or snowboarding, many activities open us up to incredible areas of physical experience that are much more fascinating than what the churches have to offer.

Are you talking in terms of sports as a substitute for religion?

Why talk in terms of a substitute? There's potentially just as much religiosity in in-line skating or hang-gliding as in a church service. In the course of our discussions, I often repeat a phrase to characterize the spirituality I attempt to convey: "Religion is our life and living our lives is actually religion." I'm aware that this phraseology will meet with resistance, but the truth is that our bodies are much closer to our true essence than our intellects. There's a religiosity imbedded in our bodies that cannot be found in the culture of piety found in the churches. But it *should* also be found in the churches, and that's why I'm asking myself in what ways our religious lives as Christians can be enriched by such a physical component. I'm particularly hopeful here in the case of women.

Why women? Do women tend more toward an embodied spirituality than men?

I've been able to ascertain repeatedly that women tend to be more open to mystical experience than men. I suspect this has to do with how women are more holistically disposed than men. And when they live out this holistic aspect, they are closer to the transpersonal sphere than most men. Incidentally, this situation is corroborated on the physical level by the fact that women think much more with both halves of the brain than men, who mostly activate the right side or intellectual half of their brains. Women thus allow other psychic levels to flow directly into their ways of living and styles of thinking. If we consider this unity of living and thinking to be a specifically "feminine" trait, we must mourn an overall lack of femininity in Western society. I don't mean to say that all men should become more "feminine." I'm speaking more in terms of a transformation of our fundamental life orientation. We need to get away from a one-sided fixation on money, power, success, prestige, and accomplishment and move toward a more holistic lifestyle where emotions and the body also have a place.

Could you please explain the concept of "feminine" in more concrete terms?

Femininity has to do with intuition, feelings, openness, and a more holistic apprehension of the world. It's also connected with seeing, sensitivity, attention, devotion, and love. These feminine elements have become overly infiltrated with foreign influences in our patriarchal age, resulting in conserving and caring qualities being ignored, if not debased. Feminine elements hardly have a chance to have a formative influence in our development in society. Women are torn between the two fields of private life and business life, although they could actually act as a connecting rod between the two fields of "I" and "We." Communicating between these two is one of the greatest tasks facing present society. We're still totally caught up in a narcissistic egoism that is basically masculine in character. If we don't want to lose ourselves in the process, we must regain the "we" element that has been lost and which ascribes more meaning to a

xxviiiIntroduction

feminine worldview. This starts with care, respect for humanity and nature, the ability to listen, a group feeling, and joy in the organization, and goes on to include a fairer market economy and socialization of capitalism. Creativity, joy in living, and delight in the finer things of life, such as art and other life-affirming aspects, could help to humanize the barren landscape of business, management, and economics. But I don't place my main hopes in the feminist movements. It's more a matter of an *inner* change that we could characterize in the modern idiom as a transformation, an integration of interior and exterior values.

And if I understand you correctly, our churches should make a start here. What concrete steps can the churches take to discover a more holistic religiosity?

When it comes to feminine aspects of religiosity, a possible start would be a rediscovery of the body. In our house in Würzburg, we have had considerable success with prayer gestures. Such gestures make possible a form of spiritual service in which people do not simply sit in pews but also bring their bodies actively into the rituals. With prayer gestures and/or meditative dancing, the body becomes a medium of religious communication. Thus, it is possible to restore religiosity to our daily lives which has been lost to corporeality. I've co-authored a book with Beatrice Grimm entitled, *Heaven Is in You,*[1] which attempts to make up for precisely this lack in modern spirituality.

Would you say, following your thesis, that mysticism and such elements as the body, spirituality, and everyday life are not mutually exclusive?

On the contrary, they infuse one another. In that connection I like to quote the German artist Josef Beuys: "The mystery is happening in the train station." That's how it really is. God manifests himself in everyday life, and that's the only place we're going to find him. Meister Eckhart (1260–1327) expressed this truth most vividly in his highly original interpretation of the story of Mary and Martha in the Bible. It is not Mary—sitting in ecstasy at Jesus' feet—who is our model, but Martha, slaving away in the kitchen to serve Jesus a meal. Martha is further along the spiritual path than Mary. She is no stranger to mystical experience and allows her everyday life to be informed by that experience, while Mary still indulges in the joys of spiritual ecstasy. Mary still has to make the journey through her enlightenment experience in order to return to everyday life. It is there, in the simple things of life, that we experience the divine reality. God does not want to be praised, God wants to be *lived.* The single reason we're born as human beings is that God wants to become human in us.

In other words, we should understand everyday life as an exercise or practice, as Karlfried Graf Durckheim expressed it.

In my own case, at least, I'm attempting to rediscover and take account of the inherent religiosity in many of our everyday activities that still have a physical element. That means bringing something to in-line skating and snowboarding that will allow them to be recognized as forms of religious expression just as much as prayers recited in church. It is only in the here-and-now, in the present moment, that we have the possibility of communicating with what is truly real. It doesn't matter who you are. There is the classic comment by Meister Eckhart:

> Do all you do, acting from the core of your soul, without a single "Why." I tell you, whenever what you do is done for the sake of the kingdom of God, or for God's sake, or for eternal blessing, and thus really for ulterior motives, you're wrong. You may pass for a good person, but this is not the best. For, truly, if you imagine that you're going to get more out of God by means of religious offices and devotions, in sweet retreats and solitary orisons, than you might by the fireplace or in the stable, then you might just as well think you could seize God and wrap a mantle around his head and stick him under the table! To seek God by rituals is to get the ritual and lose God in the process, for he hides behind it. On the other hand, to seek God without artifice is to take him as

he is, and so doing, a person "lives by the Son" and is Life itself. For if Life were questioned a thousand years and asked: "Why live?" and if there were an answer, it could be no more than this: "I live only to live!" And that is because Life is its own reason for being, springs from its own Source, and goes on and on, without ever asking why—just because it is life. Thus, if you ask a genuine person, that is, one who acts from his heart: "Why are you doing that?"—he will reply in the only possible way: "I do it because I do it!"[2]

But a prerequisite would be to make it possible to experience our embodiment in church services and prayer services.

Yes. Through a mutual saturation of the body and religion, our everyday lives could take on a new religious dimension. You could also say that everyday life is prayer. I'm in the habit of telling my students after a meditation course: "The past days have been a kind of training for everyday life. You have been practicing for life. Every step you take is a continuation of this course. Walking is prayer and prayer is walking, for it can also be experienced as a means of expressing the divine reality." Standing can also be a prayer, or each time we wait for the bus. In this connection I'm fond of recounting a traditional Hassidic story:

The rabbi's students asked him what the secret of his wisdom was. He answered: "When I sit, I sit; when I stand up, I stand up; when I walk, I walk." The students exchanged embarrassed glances, imagining they hadn't heard their teacher right. So they asked him again: "Master, what is the secret of your wisdom?" Once again he said, "When I sit, I sit; when I stand up, I stand up; when I walk, I walk." The students became restless and said, "Master, that which you say, we also do, but we are far indeed from your wisdom." The rabbi smiled and shook his head. "No," he said, "when you sit, you've already stood up; when you stand up, you're already on your way; and when you walk, you've already arrived!"

And here you've touched on a specific problem. The anecdote seems to suggest that you have to be a wise rabbi to find "the mystery at the train station," to use Josef Beuys' words.

The mutual diffusion of everyday life and spirituality presupposes an experience of how everything can be a means of expressing the divine. In that sense, living our lives is the actual content of religiosity. All prayers and rituals are simply something we add to it in order to celebrate that truth. It's important, nonetheless, to recognize that living our lives is our actual religious duty. That doesn't necessarily mean being a wise rabbi. You only have to be ready to set out on the spiritual path.

Generally speaking, however, people don't understand spirituality and mysticism as diffusion in everyday life but as the opposite: otherworldliness and asceticism.

Abandoning old habits and attachments is an initial step on the spiritual path, but it's not asceticism for its own sake: it's liberation from our conditioning. That step is absolutely necessary, but equally necessary is the return to the everyday world, although that world will be experienced in a totally new and different way. Here I'd like to recount another short anecdote:

A woodcutter was cutting wood on the edge of the forest, making his living from the wood he cut. When a hermit happened to pass by one day, the woodcutter asked the hermit for a motto for his life. The hermit said, "Go deeper into the woods!" The man took his axe and went deeper into the forest. There he found wonderful trees, which he cut down and sold for a good price, becoming wealthy in the process. One day he remembered the words of the hermit: "Go deeper in the woods!" So he set off again and found a vein of silver. He mined the silver and became very rich. Several years later he once again remembered the words of the hermit: "Go deeper into the woods!" He went yet deeper into the forest and found wonderful jewels, a symbol of enlightenment. He was

beside himself with joy, but then once again the words of the
hermit occurred to him: "Go deeper into the woods." He set
out again and went deeper into the forest. With the result
that, one morning, he found himself precisely on that edge
of the woods where he had met the hermit many years before as he was cutting wood!

What does this story tell us? It tells us that anyone who travels a
spiritual path returns eventually as a changed a person back in everyday life. The following words are ascribed to the Sixth Patriarch
Hui-neng (638–713) in the Zen tradition: "How wonderful, I cut wood
and carry water!" In the Gnostic Gospel of Thomas, Jesus says, "Split
a piece of wood, and I am there. Pick up a stone and you will find me
there."

*In attempting to sum up what we've been discussing thus far, we come
up with the following overall picture. We are living in a "threshold situation" where, due to society's rapid transformation, more and more
people experience a crisis in which they no longer find any meaning in
their lives. At the same time, this can often induce them to set out on a
spiritual journey, or at least to feel a growing spiritual longing. Now
there is the old idea, especially attributed to Joachim of Fiore (1135–
1202), that the third millennium will be a millennium of the Spirit.
Keeping in mind Karl Rahner's famous dictum that the Christian of
the future will be a mystic or nothing at all, are we on the threshold of a
spiritual era?*

"The person of the future will be a mystic." If we understand
Joachim of Fiore's vision in that way, then I agree completely. Although I'm not fond of speculating on what will happen in the next
thousand years, I could say in more modest terms that the twenty-
first century will be a metaphysical century. The driving force will
no longer be the philosophers and theologians, however—it will be
the scientists. They are the ones who clearly point to a reality that we
can no longer prove rationally. In other words, they point to what all
religions up to now have rightly referred to as God. It's true that we

find ourselves in a situation of radical change. I sense that we are
now at the cusp of an accelerated evolution of the human species,
the direction of which, however, we still cannot discern.

*In other words, you're envisaging a sort of progress in the evolution
of the human species. What will be the driving force behind that
progress?*

There are capabilities still lying dormant in us. Up to now, our
potential has only been activated to the extent necessary for the survival of the species. If the conditions for survival change, we can expect a new, unknown potential to be released, much in the same way
that certain abilities more highly developed in particular ethnic groups
are barely present in the majority of people. For example, there's a
study by Dr. Marlo Morgan, a woman who lived for three months
with Australian aborigines. She says she could observe abilities among
them that were necessary for the survival of the community and which
therefore underwent marked development. They included telepathy,
homeopathy, and the ability in old age, when their lives had run their
course, to "breathe out" the spirit in a very short time. We westerners
are like pianists tinkling away on a single octave. But a piano has
seven octaves! That means we're only using the most elementary spiritual senses, while an unknown potential remains dormant in the
depths of our shared consciousness that will enable us to apprehend
and interpret reality in totally different ways. This potential, in its
various forms, will be of the greatest significance for the survival of
our species if the conditions for life on this planet continue to change
as quickly and dramatically as they have in the past one hundred
years. How will we respond when new technologies flood the earth,
when it becomes possible to clone people and create robots that will
devalue the worth of human workers, when the world population
exceeds the ten billion mark? It would not be particularly logical to
assume that the mental capacity we have possessed up to now will be
sufficient in dealing with such problems. Our only hope lies in evolutionary progress, in the human consciousness, so that the ability
emerges in the species to set free new potential in our consciousness,

and that there is enough time left to do so. Our consciousness has been undergoing a process of further development.

Notes

1. Willigis Jäger and Beatrice Grimm, *Der Himmel in Dir* (Kösel Verlag, 2000).

2. *Meister Eckhart: A Modern Translation*, by Raymond Bernard Blakney (New York: Harper and Row, 1941), 127.

PART ONE

The Foundations
of Mystical Spirituality

CHAPTER 1

The Wave Is the Ocean

What Mystical Experience Is in Its Essence

For many people, the word mysticism *has a ring of the irrational or mysterious to it, at least not something for educated persons of our modern age. How do you react to such conjectures?*

It's true enough that the image of mysticism is vastly distorted in the West. There's an unpleasant taste of bigotry and exoticism still clinging to the word, if not downright mystification and a sort of elitist sanctity. But that is precisely what mysticism is not. And for that very reason it's important at the outset to make clear what mysticism actually is: nothing less than the realization of reality.

The realization of reality? Are you saying reality has to be "realized" again?

Strange as it sounds, that's exactly what I'm saying. The reality we consider to be real is not the real reality. The real reality only opens itself to us when we leave behind our everyday ego-consciousness and enter a higher sphere of consciousness. This sphere of consciousness can be characterized as opposed to the personal consciousness, or "ego-sphere." It can be defined as the transpersonal consciousness.

Mystical experience, according to your thesis, is something like a leap to a higher level of consciousness. What's involved in all these levels of consciousness?

We find a differentiation among levels of consciousness in the writings of many proponents of advanced psychology. Jean Gebser (1905–1973), for example, was a pioneer in investigating the development of human consciousness. We also find a very differentiated analysis of the spectrum of consciousness in the work of the American researcher Ken Wilber (born 1949), who distinguishes among a prepersonal, personal, and transpersonal level. The transpersonal level is further divided into the layers of the subtle, causal, and cosmic consciousness. The prepersonal or prerational level of consciousness is the level of physical and sensory perception, of the emotions, simple pictorial and symbolic cognition and mystical ideas, without any clear realization. On the personal level of consciousness, we're dealing with our ego-consciousness. It is our everyday consciousness with its clear reasoning and logic. It is the level of the sciences and conceptual understanding of the world. On the transpersonal level of consciousness, we transcend our ego-consciousness. We enter a subtle reality that transcends our ego. It is the level of pictures and symbols, of visions and prophecies. On the causal level it comes to an experience of unity with an "other"—a personal God, for example, regardless of whether we call it Parusha, Brahma, Yahweh, or Allah.

What happens on the level of the cosmic or transpersonal consciousness?

It's on the level of cosmic consciousness that actual mystical experience takes place. It involves an experience of emptiness, of God without a predicate. On this level we experience "pure existence," the source from which all things issue. It is the level that precedes everything that can happen. The mystical experience is an experience of the oneness of form and emptiness, an experience of the unity of our own identity with the primary reality. This state of consciousness is the goal of the spiritual path. It is the mystical experience, and persons who experience it will never be the same. Their ideas of religion will have been transformed. To take this step into the mystical is in a sense a dying to self. And for that reason it is also known as the "death of the ego" in the mystical tradition.

It sounds as if the ego were something bad that we have to rid ourselves of.

That's not what is meant. Mysticism doesn't want to conquer the ego or fight with it. It simply wants to show the ego its limits, to attribute to it the importance it deserves, yet no more. Thus, mysticism attempts to see the ego for what it really is: an organizational center for the personal structure of each individual. It's what makes human beings what we are. That's a matter of course in mysticism. However, the mystical experience brings us to the point where we can no longer identify simply with our superficial ego. We are thus liberated for a reality where the ego is no longer dominant.

But aren't you giving short shrift to the very foundations of Western thinking with such a statement? We westerners attribute much more importance to the ego than is true in the East. There would seem to be a difference here between the two spiritual traditions.

It's not so much a difference between Eastern and Western spirituality as between mystical and nonmystical spirituality. You find statements in Meister Eckhart or John of the Cross that point in the same direction as those of Eastern wisdom teachers. For mystics, the ego is a conglomerate of conditionings that we have acquired in the course of our lives. Over the years we create an identity that we call "I." Also playing a role here are such aspects as our home and upbringing, schooling, religion, society, spouse, friends, ideals, fears, desires, prejudices, illusions, and so on. We identify with this collection of patterns. We defend our ego with anger or fear. We judge it and condemn it in ourselves and in others. We are both proud of it and guilty about it. This serves to strengthen the illusion of a separate self. But the ego actually has no substance. Composed of acquired constructs, it is actually only a "function center" used by our true essence like an instrument. It will disappear when we die. What remains is our true, divine identity. It is not important to me whether an individual continuum remains after death. What persists is divine life, which is neither born nor dies. That is our true identity.

And that makes mysticism a matter of experience?

In mysticism we realize that the ego is just as much a manifestation of the original reality as anything else. But due to the fact that it *experiences* itself as a reality above the others, the ego is not "less me" but rather "more me." Thus, mystics do not experience the loss of their ego as a loss. The experience is something so much more precious that any thoughts of loss fade away in insignificance. For this reason, mystics, in most cases, have strong personalities. Many of the mystics of the past had such a strongly developed sense of self that they were ready to be burned at the stake rather than be untrue to their convictions.

But people of today would hardly be prepared to subordinate their ego. Our whole worldview, our whole feeling of being alive and the structure of our society attribute the greatest possible importance to the ego. How can such a spirit of the times be consistent with the way of mysticism as you've described it?

It is not only the spirit of our times that attributes so much importance to the ego. Religious education over the centuries has also led us to believe that we have to behave in a particular way to be justified before God, whether it be with good works or unshakable faith. In both cases we are required to achieve something for the sake of our ego. Mysticism, on the other hand, says: Do away with all desires to achieve something. According to mysticism, life is not a matter of justification, self-satisfaction, or self-realization. It is simply a matter of perceiving intentions motivated by the ego—even, or more especially, the religious intentions—as being conditioned by time. Contemplative practice involves subordinating the will, even granted our intentions are perfectly good. As long as we engage in religious practices or profess belief in order to achieve something, we are not yet on the way of mysticism. We are still stuck in the schema of *do ut des,* or "I give, in order that you may give." I do not say this in criticism of the will itself. But it explains the inability of the will to transcend the purely personal sphere.

That isn't very sympathetic with the general ethic of our times, which puts a lot of emphasis on what we have achieved.

True enough, although it would be overly simplistic to just criticize the spirit of our times without realizing how it is following a tendency that is found in all established religions: the tendency to leave its stamp on structures which then pave the way for what amounts to a spiritual version of the barter economy. Whenever ethical norms are enacted and creeds are extolled as our salvation, the temptation is all too strong to use those norms and creeds to pacify the ego. Far from helping us let go of the ego, they have the opposite effect of anchoring the ego even more strongly. And that's not all. The ego is caught in a prison of its own making.

That sounds like a criticism of religion.

Religions have various levels, each with its own justification. It's simply a shame when we remain on one of those levels and consider it to be the whole of it. But that is precisely what happens when the ego contents itself with following ethical guidelines and tenets of faith in a religion and requires others to do the same. On the spiritual path of mysticism, however, all that is left behind. The mystical way leads us to a transconfessional level where the statement "I believe" becomes a certainty to the extent that we have experienced it, and where fixation on the ego recedes. Although the truths remain the same, they are interpreted variously on each step along the way. This is true for all religions, whether Buddhism or Hinduism, Islam or Christianity.

If I understand you correctly, this crossover from the confessional to the transconfessional level is synonymous with the ascent from a personal to a transpersonal consciousness. You've also characterized this transformation as an awakening from a semi-twilight state to actual reality. How do we bring all these elements together?

Reality appears to us in another light, depending on what level of consciousness we are on. I can add here that we recognize a higher level of consciousness by the fact that everything we considered to be the entire truth is seen to be only part of the truth. Most people have been on an intellectual or mental level since the Age of Enlightenment. Characteristic of that level is the strong dominance of an ego-consciousness, which imagines there is an objective world that can be perceived and controlled by reason. A striking example is the theism we spoke about earlier. In its crassest forms, it manifests itself in our modern scientistic-positivistic worldview. People who live their lives on this level are content to explain all life processes in terms of chemistry, physiology, and/or psychology.

Does that mean a scientistic worldview does not give full justice to reality?

According to the positivists, the pivot of human existence is the brain, which produces consciousness as a result of complex neurological processes. Mysticism, on the other hand, claims the opposite: It's not the brain that produces consciousness; it's rather consciousness that creates forms for itself in addition to a brain. According to that view of things, we are not primarily complex biochemical and cellular structures, but spirit—spirit that gives itself one possible form in the mental ego-consciousness, although it is by no means exhausted in that form. The intellect is one particular manifestation of spirit, and the brain is nothing more than a material condensation or intensification of spiritual energy. However, beyond its manifestations and concentrations, this spiritual reality experiences itself in the mystical experience. It is here that the spirit "becomes aware of itself," so to speak, although it is still separated from itself on the level of reason with its subject-object dualism.

And mysticism resolves that dualism?

The mystical level of consciousness is transpersonal. On that level, there is no longer an ego that asserts itself as an independent subject in dualistic opposition to an objective world. Now it experiences itself in unity with that world while containing an added value. None of this has very much to do with mysticism. It agrees essentially with the findings of modern science. No one is expected to believe in something totally fantastic or incomprehensible. However, anyone who denies that there is such a level of consciousness has already blocked the way to mysticism at the outset. It won't be possible to convince such a person with logical arguments. Mysticism is not a matter of faith, but of experience. The psychoanalyst C. G. Jung hit the nail on the head when he wrote:

> Religious experience is absolute, it can't be discussed. One can only say that one has never had such an experience. Then one's opponent will say, "Sorry, but I have," thereby ending the discussion. It doesn't matter what the world thinks about religious experience: the person who has it possesses the greatest treasure of a thing that has become for him a source of life, meaning, and beauty and that has given the world and the human race a new brightness.[1]

But is it beyond the realm of possibility, then, to convince people of the reality of a transpersonal sphere of consciousness?

Christianity holds up the concept of grace for this. In this way, a person who thinks in purely materialistic terms will not be shaken from the outside. How could he? He is lacking the "sensory antenna," so to speak, for the mystical dimension. To talk to such a person about that dimension would be like attempting to explain colors to a blind person. The transmental reality cannot be perceived with mental means—and that's all we have to work with when talking to people who are stuck on the mental level. You can never convince someone of the reality of the spirit, you can't make arguments on its behalf. The door has to be opened from the inside, as it were. As we've seen already, it's similar to when our entire worldview comes into question in a life crisis.

Does this amount to giving up a positivistic view of reality?

No, but it could be called giving up ignorance. We're talking about one of the greatest examples of folly that humanity has ever allowed itself to be carried away with. Hard-boiled positivists only hurt themselves when they insist on closing their eyes to the fact that reality is broader and richer than what we can measure, weigh, or count. Hans-Peter Dürr, someone who could hardly be accused of being an opponent of science, once said:

> What science helps me do is realize its limits. The layperson has a much more optimistic idea of what you can understand with science. What science teaches me is to see the limits of scientific thinking. That doesn't mean throwing science overboard.... We're all connected to those sources out of which the answers must eventually come.[2]

And that source is the transmental sphere of consciousness.

You said that fixation on the mental level is a modern phenomenon. That gives the impression that humanity as a whole has passed through various stages of consciousness.

And will no doubt be passing through others in the future. There really is an evolution of consciousness, as has been shown by Jean Gebser, Ken Wilber, and others. We originally came from an archaic preconsciousness and developed ourselves further in a magical consciousness. We still find traces of that former level of consciousness in the mythical traditions of ancient cultures, in fairy tales, and among ethnic groups existing today that have been studied by ethnologists. But then humanity came to a point where it was no longer possible to interpret and understand itself, let alone the world, on that level of consciousness. As a result, consciousness advanced to a mystical level. Now there was a heaven with gods dwelling there—or perhaps just a single god—who organized and protected the world. To sum up: Religions have developed in the way that they still form and influence the lives of many people even today. But the time when a religious-mythical consciousness could encompass all facets of life was already over. A further level of consciousness had been reached: the mental consciousness, which has dominated our world and our self-understanding for several generations by now. However, we now experience how the formation and further development of our mental abilities bring us to a limit. We've reached a threshold that we can possibly extend—thanks to our scientific and technological understanding—but which we can never cross with logic alone. We've reached a point where we are forced to release a potential that lies dormant in us so as to experience more of what reality actually is. This liberation of the dormant capabilities of consciousness lies in the transpersonal sphere of consciousness. It is mysticism.

That makes it sound as if mysticism were the latest or perhaps final product of an evolution of consciousness already thousands of years old. That's a little disturbing to hear, considering how most known testimony of the great mystics is already several hundred years old. The Buddha lived twenty-five hundred years ago and Meister Eckhart about eight hundred years ago.

Yes, that's true, although it's no argument against believing in an evolution of consciousness. If we assume that our spirit has been endowed with a mystical capacity since the beginning of humankind, it's only natural to assume that there were individuals scattered throughout history who were something like forerunners of mystical experience. Seen as a whole, their numbers were very few. There are no signs in history that humanity, in general, has ever characterized itself through a mystical understanding. Nevertheless, there are indications that humanity is on the way toward such an understanding.

And what would they be?

Human consciousness, as Jean Gebser ascertained in his research, has continued to develop. Our solar system came into existence some 4.5 billion years ago. About 600 million years ago the first forms of life appeared on the earth. Approximately 370 million years ago, the first reptile emerged from the water, becoming the ancestor of the vertebrates. About 3 million years ago, humans developed from one of the primates. Why should this development cease at this point?

We've already spoken at length about mystical experiences. You've also mentioned that we actually can't talk about such an experience because it is encountered on a level of consciousness that cannot be adequately conveyed with the mental tools of language, conceptualism, and logic. Nevertheless, mystics have always attempted the impossible, clothing their experiences in words and pictures. Can I ask you to make a similar attempt?

Let me begin by saying that, although it's true that mystics always make use of pictures and symbols, those pictures and symbols always come *after* an experience. There is the statement by the Chinese master Foyan (1067–1120): "If people use words to describe the Mind, they have not understood the Mind; but if they attempt to describe the Mind without using words, they also don't understand the Mind."

Why is that so?

Because all our pictures, symbols, and words undergo a process of continual change, while the divine remains unchanged. Here are the words of Meister Eckhart on the subject: "If I had a God whom I could realize, I would never take him to be God." You can understand why John of the Cross said about God: "Nada, nada," that is, "Not this and not that." You can't say anything more about God. The mystics in all religions are unanimous on this point. That's why we recite in a Zen text by Master Daio Kokushi (1232–1308): "There is a reality that precedes heaven and earth. It has no form, let alone a name. Eyes cannot see it when they seek it. It has no voice and cannot be heard by ears." And he continues: "My worthy friends, if you desire to hear the thunderous voice of the Dharma, give up your words, empty your thoughts. Then you may come to the point of realizing the single being."

That means we should take heed of Ludwig Wittgenstein's famous dictum: "About that which we cannot speak, we should remain silent."

The only way out of this dilemma, as mentioned already, is found in metaphors, parables, and pictures, while keeping in mind that they only offer us an access to those mystical truths. Here's an image I like to make use of: If we consider the primary reality to be an endless ocean, then we are something like the waves on that ocean. When the wave experiences that "I am the ocean," there are still two: wave and ocean. In mystical experience, however, even this duality is transcended. The "I" of the wave becomes blurred, and instead the ocean experiences itself as wave. It experiences itself *in* the unity of both and *as* the unity of both. The mystic does not take this step, the step happens to him. He no longer views reality as his opposite, as something outside of himself; he experiences reality from within. To return to our image of the wave and the ocean: He experiences that everything is simultaneously wave and ocean. Everything is an expression of this single reality. And because everything is an expression of the same reality, there is an absolute connection with everything. The ocean is all waves and all waves are a unity. Everything is the cosmos and everything in the cosmos is a manifestation of the same cosmic being. But the mystic experiences this in the fact that all differences between him and the manifestations of being disappear. Mysticism is not *beyond* God and the world. Mysticism *is* God and the world, an indissoluble unity. Thus, the tension between the two poles is not removed. It is like the tension on both ends of the staff. It is the tension between wave and ocean, between branch and tree. For this reason, God and the human being are not equated with each other. The ocean reveals itself as ocean. Ocean and wave can be addressed separately, but their essence is water. My hand has two sides. If you examine it with normal logic, you have to examine each side in succession. From within, however, both sides are experienced as one. It is thus an experience of total emptiness and total fullness.

The word emptiness *sounds negative in the ears of many people. For them, the word* emptiness *is an emotive word of Eastern spirituality that they play off against the personal encounter with God in Western mysticism.*

Emptiness is the gateway, not the goal. The goal is always emptiness *and* form, as it is expressed in Zen. Nirvana doesn't mean dissolving into an undifferentiated soup. Nirvana is the experience of the here-and-now and not some state in the distant future. Emptiness is not empty! We must dispense with three prejudices against Eastern mysticism. The first is the accusation that it remains stuck in emptiness. In Zen, you would call such a state "dead Zen." We can speak just as well about "fullness" as of "emptiness." In this fullness there is no existence for itself, but the experience of cosmic "being with." All mystics attest to this experience. Thus, Meister Eckhart writes:

When one takes God as he is, divine, having the reality of God within him, God sheds light on everything. Everything will taste like God and reflect him. God will shine in him all the time. He will have the disinterest, renunciation, and spiritual vision of his beloved, ever-present Lord.[3]

And Ramana Maharishi (1879–1950) says regarding the enlightened one: "The one perceiving perceives directly through the awareness of God." Ecstasy, rapture, and visions are not the goal of mysticism. All of these are only the gateway. John of the Cross explains this in no uncertain terms:

Thus we have raptures and transports and the dislocation of bones, which always occur when the communications are not purely spiritual (communicated to the spirit alone) as are those of the perfect, who are already purified by the night of spirit. The perfect enjoy freedom of spirit without their senses being clouded or transported, for in them these raptures and bodily torments cease.[4]

You mentioned a second prejudice.

We should also stop accusing Eastern mysticism of propagating self-salvation. Salvation in mysticism is to "perceive" or "realize" the truth, a state given to those who can let go. It is only in letting go that we realize the eternally present reality "undarkened" by the ego; it is never of our own doing. We Christians have been far more exhorted to earn heaven through good works.

What is the third prejudice concerning Eastern mysticism?

It's the assumption that a mystical experience is subjective. The only subjective element is the representation or expression of the experience. Anyone who has had a deep mystical experience has realized the one and true essence behind all verbalization and symbolic representation, provided those words and pictures actually describe such an experience. I have a book of 1200 haiku (Japanese verse form consisting in three lines containing five, seven, and five syllables respectively). Although the poems are very different in content, this element of essential oneness shines through unmistakably, and that is what is encountered in a mystical experience. No one can fake something that he hasn't actually experienced. Unpardonably obtuse is the claim regarding mysticism that we end up in a situation where everyone has his or her own religion. Actually, however, the One is experienced and, according to the individual person, expressed in an unmistakable way.

Can you speak of your own experiences, in view of what you've just said?

I'd like to familiarize you with experiences of people traveling the spiritual path under my guidance. Please don't forget that this always involves a description after the fact. Thus, although the word *I* appears repeatedly, there is no "I" to speak of in the actual experience. You could speak in terms of "emptiness that is not empty, and from which sounds, colors, feelings, and thoughts come." It is a meta- or supracosmic emptiness. The ego and emptiness have flowed together. Emptiness, divinity—or "nada," in the words of John of the Cross—can also be referred to as "fullness." It is the fullness pregnant with myriad possibilities. It contains all capabilities and is both origin and creation. It is coming home to our original home where nothing is lacking: Laughing, but not laughing about something, just laughing; happy, but not happy about something; limitless love, but no "I love you." Paradoxically, there is neither love nor hate here, neither life nor death, neither you nor me, no boundaries, no space, no time. *It* walks along with lightness, matter-of-factness, and freedom. All polarity is gone. Nothing is absurd; on the contrary, everything is fully natural. There is the beating of the drum. The individual tones drop out of nothingness like pearls, only to disappear again. No inside, no outside. A swig of juice, just that intense taste. Walking, just this step. *It* walks, *It* sees, *It* feels, and, as crazy as it sounds, *It* thinks. Even thoughts bubble up out of nowhere and disappear. It is my experience, but this experience shows itself in everything that I am saying here or have ever written. That's why my words often sound unusual. That's why they are also hard to understand from time to time. They come from another level of experience. And even when I say that, it has nothing to do with spiritual elitism. Nevertheless, I cannot speak otherwise without denying my own experience.

Does what you're saying agree with what we traditionally refer to as unio mystica?

Yes. *Unio mystica* is the Christian term for this descent into cosmic, transmental, and transpersonal oneness. Other names have been coined for the same experience in other religions and cultures: emptiness, enlightenment, liberation, *satori, nirvana, samadhi,* and so on. Regardless of the words used, it is always the same experience of pure existence in which everything is as it is, and also perfect as it is. But this pure existence is not some sort of substance. Here you are neither happy nor unhappy, neither satisfied nor dissatisfied, neither joyful nor sad. Saying "I'm happy" would already be tantamount to falling back to the level of the ego. In the cosmic consciousness there is no bliss, there is no happiness in the sense of a feeling. Feelings are always the feelings of a separate "I." Here it is a case of *just* happiness, without "I'm happy." It is ecstasy, but not "I'm ecstatic." For anyone who has transcended the ego, all other levels of consciousness seem relative, while the cosmic consciousness is self-contained and perfect as it is, completely fulfilled. It is the fulfillment of all our longings. Why shouldn't it be the goal of all existence? Why shouldn't we refer to it as "heaven"?

Some people claim that the Christian mystical experience has elements superior to the spirituality of other religions. You wouldn't agree with them?

No, I would not. When I read the poems of John of the Cross, I can't find any difference from mystical experiences in other religions. There are two poems of his that I want to cite for special attention: "I entered into unknowing" and "How well I know the source." You don't find anything personal or specifically Christian in these texts. That's why John Chapman (1865–1933)—a Christian spiritual director and wonderful counselor and companion for people on the spiritual path—could write: "Saint John of the Cross is like a sponge full of Christianity. You can squeeze it all out, and the full mystical theory remains. Consequently, for fifteen years or so, I hated John of the Cross and called him a Buddhist. I loved Saint Teresa, and read her over and over again. She is first a Christian, only secondarily a mystic. Then I realized that—as far as prayer was concerned—I had wasted fifteen years." John of the Cross has accompanied me on my own spiritual journey over the decades. I agree wholeheartedly with this statement of John Chapman.

So you would say that we could find the fulfillment of all our longings in all religions, even if they have found other names to refer to that fulfillment?

All religions are ways of experiencing the divine, but no religion can lay sole claim to access to God. I like to clarify this with an image: Religions are like beautifully colored stained-glass windows. They give the light that shines through them a specific structure. If there is no light, the windows are dull and meaningless. Thus it is the light that is the decisive element. But we can't see the light with our eyes. Light makes things visible, but is itself invisible. It only becomes visible when it is divided into colors and takes on a structure. This is true also about religions when considering the divine. Religions give a tangible structure to the intangible. The price that religions pay for this is the reduction of the divine to one part of its entire spectrum. It would be foolish to take that part for the whole. It would be as foolish as believing that a stained-glass window has its own power of illumination independent of the light that shines on the window and lights it up. Besides that, we need to realize that the light must be broken up into a spectrum of colors if it is to become visible and not simply shine. God appears in the religions but will never be experienced there in the total fullness of his light if the religions are not open to experience.

Does that mean, in order to directly experience what we call God, we would have to step out of the "darkness of the church" and dare to stand under the open sky?

I don't believe there is a divine realm for us beyond all structure and diffraction, if we were to pursue our image of the light in a prism. I cannot realize something that is not a facet of the One. The primary reality is always everything. God exists as form and as non-form. Just as the light is not recognizable other than in something on which it shines, there is no God for us without form. If there is nothing that the light shines on, you don't see the light either. We could even say that what we refer to as an illuminated object is nothing more than bundled light! It really is nothing more than light. The light appears when it illuminates itself. This is precisely the case with God. There exists only God, because God's very self is being. Everything that exists is an appearance of being, "bundled being," so to speak. This is what the mystic experiences. He does not experience the pure, naked God beyond all religions. He does not step outside the church door to look in the sun. (He would ruin his eyes in the process, as Plato says in his parable of the cave!) Rather, he experiences that everything, including himself, is an appearance of God—a "bundling" of divine being. The cosmos is an epiphany of God. Thus true mysticism transcends teachings of karma. Cause and effect are ways in which the divine appears. If there is rebirth, then we would have to say: It is only this divine original principle that is reborn. But neither the mysticism of the East nor that of the West speaks about rebirth. It is the present moment—the here-and-now—that is the timeless moment of God. A while back someone accused me of degrading humanity to the level of a continuous-flow water heater. That person had yet to realize that we are also what flow through the water heater!

How should we understand that statement?

God and the human species are in a relationship to each other like gold and a ring. They are two completely different realities. The gold is not the ring and the ring is not the gold. But in a golden ring they can only appear together. They are coexistent. The gold needs a form to appear, and the ring needs a material to become visible. They are "not-two." As the gold reveals itself as ring, so God reveals himself as the human species. They can only appear together. This, for me, is the meaning of the Incarnation of Christ. Through that particular incarnation it should be made apparent that everything represents an incarnation of God, from quarks and leptons to purely spiritual forms that we have no idea about. We are "god-beings." I could also say: God has manifested himself in the human species.

We ourselves are God?

Yes, even if that sounds scandalous, if not heretical and presumptuous, in the ears of many a Christian. But that is due to the assumption that a mystic is making such a statement out of his ego-consciousness. Actually, however, it emerges from this experience of unity where there is no longer any "I and Thou." The suspicion of heresy also comes from the idea that Christianity understands something completely different by the word *God* than what we have just referred to as the divine, the primary reality, cosmic consciousness, or even God, if you will. Christianity understands by the word *God* something that, by its very definition, is in dualistic opposition to us. But such a theistic view of God only has meaning if we are acting on the rational level of consciousness. It is only there that we need a God who saves us in a particular way. From the mystical perspective this teaching of salvation is a metaphor for what occurs in mystical experience. Salvation is always "here." In the mystical experience we break through to it.

Does that mean we can bid farewell to the classical teaching of salvation?

No. Religiosity has many very different levels. Humankind will remain for a long time to come on the religious level that can only imagine salvation in terms of salvation by a savior. In saying so, I don't want to disparage or belittle this traditional view of salvation. But all believing persons should also realize that there is a level of consciousness that transcends this religious worldview. If we realize that, and the question about the meaning of life rises up in a particular life situation, we will be prepared to embark on the inner or spiritual path.

What happens then?

First, there occurs what the mystics refer to as a process of purification. In psychological terms you could also refer to it as a process of individuation in which the psyche becomes transparent for all the psychological blockages and conditioning that have developed through education, socialization, and religious education. Mind you, it's not a matter of casting aside those influences. It's more a matter of soberly assessing them and accepting them for what they are. As our soul becomes transparent, a transformation of our self-understanding occurs, especially in a religious sense. The God of heaven, to whom we prayed as children, collapses. And many will then sigh, as Nietzsche did, and say, "God is dead." Actually, however, God is not destroyed; it's more that a particular image of God has been destroyed.

This situation is a hard burden to bear for many people. They no longer know what to use for support. But in this crisis is already the departure to the next level on the inner path that begins a phase of emptying the consciousness or unifying the consciousness, according to one's religious tradition or one's environment.

What does that process of emptying involve?

On the way toward unification of consciousness we're concerned with guiding the stream of our consciousness in a particular direction. This can involve concentration on a sound, a word, or—in the Asian tradition—on a mantra. It can also involve repeating particular movements. It always involves a concentration of the consciousness, otherwise so scattered. Another approach attempts an emptying of consciousness. Here, all activity of the ego comes to rest and there is only wakeful presence. Thoughts come and go, without our attempting to hold on to them. That's not so easy, however, because our intellect is so used to directing its attention toward the impressions that flow into it, attempting to give them a structure and further develop them. Both of these methods of concentration lead us to a point where the ego realizes that it actually isn't what it considered itself to be up to then. Our ego-identification falls apart, and we realize that our actual identification lies far deeper than our ego. We are then on the threshold of the experience I attempted to describe pictorially at the outset when I said: The wave no longer experiences itself as part of the ocean, it is now only ocean—unity without an opposite.

But aren't there spiritual experiences where an opposite, an "other," appears? I recall in this connection the experiences of melting together with something else as they occur in Shamanism.

Identification with animals or other creatures, as is common in Shamanism, is no doubt a means to overcome a narrow ego-identity. But it also appears to me to be a hindrance since there is considerable danger that the initiate remains on that level and simply puts off his identification without actually coming to a mystical experience of unity. Duality cannot be overcome in this way. For example, I am presently accompanying a woman on her spiritual journey who has practiced a shamanistic way and had an experience of light that was extremely meaningful for her. But she remains fixed in that constellation, unable to leave behind her ego, which feels itself ennobled by that vision. That means she's marking time in the antechamber of the temple, so to speak, unable to take the next step toward an experience of unity.

Would you advise people to avoid shamanistic practices, in that case?

I would, at least, indicate the possible dangers involved, the greatest danger being that someone stops halfway. Incidentally, that is not only my own opinion. The great mystical traditions of the world religions warn us repeatedly against attaching too much importance to spiritual "side effects," such as telekinesis, precognition, visions, ecstasies, levitation, alleged reincarnation experiences, and the like. To be sure, such experiences can be meaningful for the individual and perhaps for a group, but they are never the final goal. And we should especially take care not to misunderstand them as a sign that we have been "chosen" in some special way. For in the final analysis, these parapsychological abilities have very little to do with genuine spirituality. It's more a matter of potentialities that everyone possesses in rudimentary form and which some can develop and others not, just as there are musically gifted people and others in whom those gifts are less developed.

Is there anything like a mystical "talent" that allows certain people to have transpersonal experiences of unity without having practiced a spiritual path?

Anyone can have such an experience unexpectedly and with no prior preparation. It's not necessary to engage in a particular spiritual practice. I'm thinking in this connection of people like Hölderlin,[5] Rilke, and Nietzsche, the last of whom evidently had something like an enlightenment experience on a crag of *Sils Maria* in Switzerland. Even his statement "God is dead" is presumably an expression of a genuine mystical experience. But the very example of Nietzsche also shows what extraordinary difficulties such unexpected breakthroughs into the transpersonal sphere can bring when we are unprepared for them. People often lack a system of coordinates wherein they can orient themselves in their experience, or they might reject a religious interpretation of the experience for ideological reasons. It would have been unthinkable for Nietzsche to interpret his existential experiences in a Christian context or any other religious context. He was in that sense a mystic who remained "stuck on the way," as it were, someone who had entered the transpersonal sphere but who then lost his way.

Could you explain that in more detail?

I'd prefer to quote a passage in Nietzsche's *Ecce Homo* referring to his experience:

I shall now tell the story of Zarathustra. The basic conception of the work, the idea of eternal recurrence, the highest formula of affirmation that can possibly be attained, belongs to August of the year 1881: it was jotted down on a piece of paper with the inscription: "6,000 feet beyond man and time." I was that day walking through the woods beside the lake of Silvaplana; I stopped beside a mighty pyramidal block of stone which reared itself up not far from Surlei. Then this idea came to me: If I think back a couple of months from this day, I find as an omen a sudden and profoundly decisive alteration in my state, above all in music....The concept of revelation, in the sense that something suddenly, with unspeakable certainty and subtlety, becomes visible, audible, something that shakes and overturns one to the depths, simply describes the fact, One hears, one does not seek; one takes, one does not ask who gives, a thought flashes up like lightning, with necessity, unfalteringly formed—I have never had any choice. An ecstasy the tremendous tension of which sometimes discharges itself in a flood of tears, while one's steps now involuntarily rush along, now involuntarily lag; a complete being outside of oneself with the distinct consciousness of a multitude of subtle shudders and trickles down to one's toes; a depth of happiness in which the most painful and gloomy things appear, not as an antithesis, but as conditioned, demanded, as a necessary color within such a superfluity of light; an instinct for rhythmical relationships which spans forms of wide extent—length, the need for a wide-spanned rhythm is almost the measure of the force of inspiration, a kind of compensation for its pressure and tension....Everything is in the highest degree involuntary but takes place as in a tempest of a feeling of freedom, of absoluteness, of power, of divinity....The involuntary nature of image, of metaphor is the most remarkable thing of all; one no longer has any idea what is image and what is metaphor, everything presents itself as the readiest, the truest, the simplest means of expression. It really does seem, to allude to a saying of Zarathustra, as if the things themselves approached and offered themselves as metaphors.[6]

Nietzsche experiences here the deep emotion of many mystics who are at first unable to fit what they have encountered into their everyday experience. It shakes them to the core. They go through heaven and hell. In the beginning it is only with great difficulty that they can bring together their ordinary way of seeing and what they have seen. Any practical application of that experience in their lives appears impossible. The individual as the bearer of conventional sensibility no longer has any meaning. And this can happen to someone who never sought it in the first place.

In Nietzsche's case, he had the intellectual power—at least initially— to clothe his experiences in words and to process them in that way. What happens, however, in the case of less creative persons when they are surprised by a mystical experience?

Since they have transcended the familiar boundaries of their ego-identity, they often fall into a threatening insecurity. This insecurity is all the greater the more the person lacks a religious framework of interpretation that allows him to integrate his experiences in his life and his religious self-understanding. Not a few persons seek psychiatric treatment because they assume they are going crazy. Even such a highly perceptive psychologist as Sigmund Freud had no real understanding of transpersonal experiences. He considered them to be abnormal and psychopathic.

That was evidently not only the case with Freud. When you examine mystical literature, it is striking how often writers describe incredible fears and periods of suffering. John of the Cross, for example, hit upon the metaphor of a "dark night" that the mystic must pass through on the way to God. Is mysticism perhaps something to fear after all?

No. What John of the Cross experienced and suffered through was a long process of purification. In an intensive study of his wonderful texts, I've repeatedly had the impression that he didn't have a very easy life, in terms of his biography. We know, for example, that he had a very difficult childhood and youth. He grew up in the narrow and threatening world of Spanish Catholicism at the time of the Inquisition. He didn't feel at home in such a milieu. There is the wonderful poem that starts with the words: "I stepped in and didn't know where." It wasn't easy for him to remain true to his experience despite the Inquisition, before which he had to appear several times. It was a process of emancipation, the difficulties of which we can hardly appreciate nowadays; he had no backing, no support, nothing he could call upon. His companion on the spiritual path, Teresa of Ávila, had it somewhat easier in this respect. She didn't hesitate to fall back on a Christian style of expression to describe her mystical experiences. John of the Cross did the same, but he is a real mystic in his poems where there is often no religious terminology at all. That was also a part of his personal "dark night."

Do you mean to say that this dark side of mysticism must not necessarily be a stage on the interior path?

Fear, terror, feelings of desolateness, and dejection in face of the "death of God" can occur in the process of the spiritual "ascent of the mountain." But they don't have to. There are not a few cases of people reaching the summit with considerable ease, and who often break into resounding laughter when they reach it. My own Zen master, Yamada Roshi (1907–1989), laughed almost continuously for three days after his decisive experience. As you can imagine, his wife thought he had gone crazy, although he hadn't. He laughed because "enlightenment" was so simple, because he simply "woke up" and saw that reality can be totally ordinary, and nevertheless perfect. In a single stroke, the whole expenditure in terms of theology, philosophy, and whatever else one studies, seems laughable. To sum up: The spiritual journey is different for each person according to his or her disposition. How that journey takes place could eventually also depend on the psychological disposition of each individual.

Based on what you're now saying, the widespread notion that mysticism is always a very serious matter is unfounded.

Yes, that view is totally unfounded. But it's also an indication of how much mysticism has been distorted in the West. Incidentally, that might also have to do with the fact that very strange criteria have been established in the Catholic Church to determine holiness or saintliness. You seldom come across pictures of laughing saints in the Catholic Church. Instead, the Church demands extraordinary morality, the ability to perform miracles, and the like from its saints. None of that has anything to do with mystical experience. It's more like a moral mail-order catalog that can't be applied to mystics. To the contrary: One of the main reasons that mystics have met with rejection is because they didn't allow themselves to be measured by the moral code of a particular time. To be sure, they conformed for the most part to the prevailing conventions and norms, although they probably realized that all of that is provisional and relative.

But aren't there also so-called "holy fools," people who disregard convention on realizing the relativity of all earthly things?

There are such people, and when they appear, they're the source of considerable discomfiture to their contemporaries. Many anecdotes about such "holy fools" have been transmitted to us from the East. An example is Zen Master Ikkyu (1394–1481) who visited brothels to convert the women there. Consider the stories of Jesus that have been handed down to us. You also find countless episodes there that must have seemed totally offensive to his contemporaries. He dined with questionable women; he communed with the very unpopular tax collectors; he even confounded his own disciples by allowing himself to be anointed with expensive oils instead of investing the money for the poor.

That sounds as if a mystical experience leads to a state where we are no longer bound in any way by social mores. Are mystics—to quote Nietzsche again—"beyond good and evil"?

The mystical experience involves a fundamental transformation of the person. It leads us to the awareness that all our moral norms are tied up at any given time with our self-understanding, which for its part depends on the level of consciousness we are on. On another transpersonal level of consciousness, our self-understanding is transformed, and with it our idea of morality. Or to put it in another way: For the person who has had a mystical experience, morality moves into the background. He or she is now filled totally with an all-embracing love of each and every person. Love becomes for that person the single determining norm, which pervades everything he or she does. For such a person, a quotation from Augustine takes on special meaning: *Ama et fac quod vis* (Love, and do what you wish.). We could add, "no matter what it is," because when your actions are imbued with the Spirit of love, they automatically fulfill everything morality prescribes and will not willfully disregard all customs and norms, since it would hardly be possible to bring that into agreement with this all-embracing love.

But what happens when moral conventions go totally against the Spirit of love?

The mystical consciousness is one of unity. Anyone who experiences himself or herself as one with others arrives at a totally new basis for morality. Love is the actual reality, and even when people have removed themselves from the experience of this primary reality, it nevertheless remains active as the creative force of evolution and the development of culture. As such, it influences the basic moral convictions of cultures and religions. Incidentally, that explains why religions—as Hans Küng attempts to show with his Global Ethic Project—hardly differ in their ethical demands.

Doesn't that mean that obedience to moral commandments necessarily leads to an experience of the divine?

No. It's true enough that Christian ethics say: "If you behave well, you will see God." But it's actually not that simple. Moral commandments can be an aid on the inner path, but they are no guarantee of mystical experience. On the contrary: There is always the danger with such moral prescriptions of binding yourself too much to moralistic disciplines and asceticism, thus remaining imprisoned in your self. It is the ego, after all, that wants to be moral, hoping in that way to go to heaven.

Seen in that way, the Protestant objection to any form of justification by works is fully justified from the mystical perspective.

That's right. Protestant criticism of the Catholic system of indulgences also has its roots here. What's problematical in Protestantism, however, is that, in the end, it is guided as much as Catholicism by the idea that "I must be justified before God." But the ego doesn't have to do that at all. The actual task of the ego is to step back and make room for the primary reality in one's life, that is, to let God come into the world. Or, as Meister Eckhart put it: "Ah, beloved people, why don't you let God be God in you? What are you afraid of?"[7]

Is this "becoming God in us" what you refer to in your books as the "sacrament of the moment"?

Yes. God happens in the here-and-now. It is only here, in this moment, that a communion and communication with God is possible. Life is the real religion; it is the fulfillment of God. God reveals himself in small things just as much as in situations that we term exalted. To communicate with God *there* is the goal of all mysticism. In prayers and rituals it is only *that* reality we are celebrating. When I celebrate the Eucharist and put bread and wine on the altar, I celebrate the unity of God and creation. Bread and wine are only exponents for the entire cosmos all the way from the atom to pure consciousness. I celebrate what has always been. The words I pronounce over the bread and wine are only confirmation, not transubstantiation. And when I baptize someone, I tell the parents and godparents: "The heavens open up here just as they did at the time of the baptism of Jesus, and a voice says: 'This is my beloved son' or 'This is my beloved daughter.'" Nothing is washed away in baptism, it is only a confirmation of what has always been there from the very beginning: the unity of God and Man.

Notes

1. *Collected Works of C.G. Jung, Volume 11: Psychology and Religion: West and East,* C.G.Jung, edited and translated by Gerhard Adler and R.F.C. Hull, (Princeton 1970), 167.
2. In W. Ebert, *Evolution, Kreativität und Bildung* (Trostberg, 1995), 149.
3. *Meister Eckhart: A Modern Translation,* by Raymond Bernard Blakney (New York: Harper and Row, 1941), 9.
4. *The Collected Works of St. John of the Cross,* translated by Kieran Kavanaugh, OCD, and Otilio Rodriguez, OCD, revised edition (ICS Publications, 1991), Book Two, 1, 2.

5. Johann Christian Friedrich Hölderlin (1770–1843) was one of the great-est German lyric poets of the romantic period, melding classical and Christian themes.
6. Friedrich Nietzsche, *Ecce Homo*, trans. by R.J. Hollingdale, Penguin Books (London, 1986), 99–103.
7. *Meister Eckhart: A Modern Translation*, by Raymond Bernard Blakney (New York: Harper and Row, 1941), 127.

CHAPTER 2

Many Paths to the One Peak

How Religions Relate to Mysticism

You said that mysticism is another name for transconfessional spirituality. That would lead us to assume that there is something like "a religion beyond religions." That sounds paradoxical. But you say it isn't. Why not?

Transconfessional spirituality does not mean a religion beyond religions, but rather a *religiosity* beyond religions. And this religiosity is a basic element of our human nature. It is a predisposition, a part of our own nature on a very deep level, to open ourselves to wholeness and oneness. We share this predisposition with all living beings; it is the driving force of evolution. Up to now, it manifested itself in the various world religions because for millenniums there was no division between religion and spirituality outside of the religions. But now we experience how this religious force breaks free from the traditional religions. I meet more and more people today who are deeply religious without professing faith in a particular religion. I take this as a sign of an ongoing evolution of consciousness.

Do you mean to say that, in the not-too-distant future, there won't be religions anymore?

That would be going too far. Religions will open themselves up. They will come to the insight that their actual goal is a spirituality transcending a particular confession. In the process they will ascertain that this transconfessionality has always been present in them. Buddha didn't want to found a religion. Neither did Jesus. It was their descendants who gave a specific form to the experience of their masters while institutionalizing it. That seems almost inevitable to me. The divine encountered in spiritual experiences strives for expression in the form of rituals and theologies. Thus there will always be—in the broadest sense—communities of believers, even when many of them will establish themselves outside the churches in the future.

Religions, in other words, are the tribute the divine must pay if it is to be experienced in the person.

Let me replace your word *tribute* with another metaphor: A religion can be compared with the Moon that illumines the Earth at night, although it receives all its light from the Sun. When the Moon comes between the Sun and the Earth, there is a solar eclipse. It's the same with religion. The Sun is the divine. It shines on the religions so they can illumine the way for us. But if a religion takes itself too seriously and comes between God and people, it "darkens" God. There is an "eclipse of God." All religions tend in that direction, and for that reason mysticism inevitably has, as part of its makeup, a certain critical stance toward organized religions. Not because it rejects religions, but as a warning against religions overstepping their bounds.

But the religious confessions, with their practices, nevertheless remain something with which many people can identify. These are traditions we have grown fond of and identities that have grown over many years. One can imagine that you meet with considerable resistance when you encourage people to bid farewell to all of that. How do you handle such situations?

I would not advise anyone to leave the religion he or she was raised in, anymore than I would like to leave my own Christian religion. But a religion is only a signpost on the way, it is not the destination. When it becomes clear to me that the signpost is taking itself too seriously and wants to hold me back on my way, I won't follow it. Of course, it's difficult for us to give up the things that seemed so natural to us since childhood. No one does such a thing unless he has started to doubt, or even despair of, that which seemed so natural up to then. That is what's happening more and more, however, as the gap grows between our present understanding of the world and the religious ideas we have inherited. I notice that the people who come to me do so in most cases because they have had a crisis of meaning. Suddenly they find themselves confronted with questions they can't answer on their own: What am I living for? Where am I going? Why did this happen to me? Religions have always attempted to give answers to those questions. But the answers no longer satisfy many people of our times. It's as if the ground suddenly vanished from under their feet, and a tremendous feeling of insecurity takes its place. It's at this point that I pick these people up, so to speak. I try to show them what an opportunity they have for a new start, whether within their religion or outside of it.

Many different ways present themselves at this point. At any rate, more and more people are turning to Eastern forms of spirituality, evidently because they believe they can satisfy their spiritual longing in that way. On the other hand, the Dalai Lama, for example, advises his European admirers to remain in their own Christian cultural milieu. Do you agree with the Dalai Lama on that point?

I consider it very important to remain in our tried-and-tested spiritual traditions. In those traditions we find understandable possibilities of interpretation and signposts along the way for everyday life as well as for how we should approach mystical experiences. Classical spiritual ways are in that respect something like maps of the Spirit that allow us to determine with considerable accuracy where we are and what lies ahead. There are certain differences, of course, among the individual spiritual paths. Each religious founder has set up his or her own signposts along the way. In the end, however, they have almost the same basic structure. All of them show the way to the same summit.

What spiritual traditions are you thinking of in that connection?

In Christianity we have the spirituality of contemplation, which has fallen into disuse for the most part. In Buddhism you have Zen and Vipassana; in Hinduism the several varieties of yoga: Krya Yoga, Raja Yoga, and Ptanjali. In Islam, Sufism has found a home and in Judaism it is the Kabbala.

How do these various spiritual ways interact with one another? Are they mutually exclusive or mutually complementary? Is it possible to practice two paths at the same time, or is it important to decide on a particular spiritual path?

All these ways are ascent routes to the same mountain summit. One way leads to the right, another to the left. One way is steeper, the other more moderate. In the end, however, they all lead to the same goal. They receive their particular stamp from the religious traditions and cultures from which they originate. The religions are—to stay with our image of the mountain—the various climatic zones that prevail on the northern, southern, eastern, or western slopes of the mountain. Anyone just starting the ascent only knows his immediate environment at first, or he only notices how the other ways differ. He does not yet suspect or sense that he will eventually ascend to a region where the various ways come closer to one another. And in the end, when he has passed through the clouds and reached the area around the summit, he sees that all the various mountainclimbers were traveling up the same mountain and had the same goal before them.

That sounds like a criticism of religion, or at least of particular confessions.

Of course I take a critical stance toward religions. I criticize in particular the fossilized or rigid, absolute structures. It was my own Christian religion that brought me to the spiritual way. I don't know where I would be today if it hadn't been for this Christian entry into the religious realm. The confessions are shelters. They are thresholds over which many people step to find their spiritual way. They have their particular value in that respect, which is not diminished by the fact that, on the spiritual path, you come sooner or later to a point where confessions are transcended. God is not really realizable in the strictures of the confessions. This does not—and I want to emphasize this point—make a case for syncretism. On the contrary, religions should prevail together. We need many "stained-glass windows" to tell us something about the light behind them. It's simply that they shouldn't make absolutes of their individual views. They should guide their adherents to the experience of what their scriptures promise. But they should not attempt to detain them in a particular confession.

But which way is right for which person?

Those who encounter the mystical way in their own religious tradition do not have to look elsewhere in other religions. However, that's extremely difficult with the forms of contemporary Christian piety. Contemplation is not taught. There are neither mystical teachers nor spiritual ways that are directed at an experience of the divine. Anyone looking for such an experience has no other choice in most cases than to look in other religious traditions. But that doesn't necessarily have to happen—which is why I'm endeavoring to unearth again the mystical heritage of Christianity and awaken it to new life. We're dealing here with treasures we've hardly dreamed of, in no way inferior to the spiritual riches of the so-called "mystical" religions of the East.

If we take a look into that treasure chest, what jewels of Western mysticism come to view?

The Greeks established the foundations for an intellectual understanding of mysticism in our cultural sphere. I've already mentioned Plato, whose philosophy provided the conceptual and metaphorical framework for the whole of Christian mysticism. But even before Plato, in the transition from the sixth to the fifth century before Christ, Parmenides had described the experience of becoming one with the divine. Following Plato, it was the Neoplatonists— in particular people like Proclus and Plotinus—who taught a mystical philosophy. They were the actual founders of the so-called *philosophia perennis*—the perennial philosophy—a tradition that was carried on by the great European mystics, such as Meister Eckhart, John of the Cross, Nicholas of Cusa, and Spinoza, to name just a few. No less important were the great women figures of mysticism: Hildegard of Bingen, Mechtild of Magdeburg, Gertrude of Helfta, Hadewijch of Antwerp, Marguerite Porete, Teresa of Ávila, and a figure like Madame Guyon. This last-mentioned person was imprisoned in the Bastille because of her mystical teachings. We don't want to forget traditional or popular mysticism as represented by Jakob Böhme and Angelus Silesius. And these are just a few names in the great history of Christian mysticism.

When we allow this truly remarkable collection of individuals to pass in revue, the question arises: Is it at all necessary to examine Buddhist or Hindu mysticism?

Study of the spiritual traditions of the East can be extraordinarily salutary and beneficial. I, for my part, was only able to realize, as a result of many years of Zen practice, that Christian mysticism essentially teaches the same thing as Zen. It was only by way of a "detour" through Japan that I was able to realize and value the treasures in my own Christian tradition.

You mentioned the "founders" of religions and said it was not their intention to found them. What is the significance of a Buddha or Jesus from a mystical standpoint?

In my view, Jesus and the Buddha are significant in the fact that they reached what we as human beings are capable of reaching: They experienced the primary reality and endeavored to convey that experience to others by showing them how they could come to the same realization. In that sense, they are like guides and companions along the inner way.

That seems to agree more or less with what is known as "imitation" in Christianity.

Yes, but there is another aspect. Many people need identification figures on the inner path, but identification figures are more than just models. We don't simply attempt to imitate them, but to become one with them in mystic contemplation. Such practices have a particular value in Tibetan Buddhism. It is a common practice in that tradition to use visualization and imagination to become one with the depiction of a divinity or *bodhisattva*. And that's not all; it is more a matter of becoming the reality represented in the depiction. Incidentally, we have something similar in the icon devotion of Orthodox Christianity. Pious Orthodox Christians understand icons as windows that allow a glimpse of the transcendental. They are likewise the link between the two levels of reality.

Assuming that we are actually on the threshold of a new phase of the evolution of consciousness or a spiritual age, will new identification figures appear, new founders of religions, new spiritual guides?

I don't expect someone to appear who could be compared with one of the great founders of the past. I have more the feeling that there will be a whole spectrum of spiritual guiding figures around which groups will develop. They will be charismatic figures who will guide other people along the way they themselves have traveled. They will be like Sherpas, who have already traveled the path and who now precede others on the way. Although new "schools" or "sects" might arise from them, that is of secondary importance. The main point is that people become spiritual adults, that they free themselves from religious leader figures. We tend to cling to the apron strings of others instead of traveling the way ourselves. Even today, not a few people are dependent on guru-like figures.

What does that mean for you as a spiritual teacher with students? Are you also a model or even an identification figure?

I hope I can avoid that danger. I've traveled a long spiritual path on which I was able to gather experiences, and I continue that journey now. I invite all those to whom this way seems reasonable to travel it with me. All those who wish to do so are welcome. Those who cannot do so should find another companion on the way.

Then you don't claim to offer the only way, or even an especially good way. But there are many other spiritual teachers beside you. Is there any competition?

There shouldn't be. A spiritual teacher will naturally attribute a special importance to the way that he or she has tried and tested. But it shouldn't come to dogmatic arguments among people who have had a genuine spiritual experience. I would go so far as to say that whenever someone claims to have the absolute truth, it's a sure sign that the person has not yet reached the abovementioned mystical sphere of consciousness.

That should provide all those searching for a spiritual teacher with a criterion for what persons to avoid. What positive criteria can you suggest to those persons?

There are no generally binding criteria that can be used to conduct a "test." I'm more in favor of the old saying: Every teacher has the students he deserves, and every student has the teacher he deserves. In the end, it is the personality and character of the teacher that determine what people will come to him or her. Only those persons will be considered whose path is attractive and practicable and who have the trust of their students. It's crucial that a relationship of trust exists between student and teacher on a spiritual path. If that is not the case, the two should mutually agree to go separate ways.

But aren't there spiritual charlatans?

Of course there are—and you can recognize them. But I want to be cautious with judgments of such persons. I go along my spiritual path and invite all those who wish to accompany me. If someone has found something better, he or she can leave at any time.

You said it's possible to recognize charlatans. How?

I become guarded, for example, when someone who advertises himself as a spiritual teacher makes too much of a show of his own person. It's also suspicious to me if he attempts to bind people to himself. Even worse is when he talks about things he has not experienced himself and cannot prove. And worst of all is when he pursues commercial gain in the process of teaching.

Many religiously motivated people seek refuge in the so-called New Age movement and in esotericism. What is the situation there regarding charlatanism and religious authenticity?

Many elements of the New Age movement do not lead to genuine mystical experience. A good deal belongs to the field of the occult, other elements to psychology or parapsychology. Of course, it's not easy to draw a precise line. For example, there are people who take drugs for altogether serious and religiously motivated reasons. In many cases they have experiences with drugs that transport them from everyday consciousness. If they have a qualified spiritual guide in such situations, the experiences can be helpful. But if it's only a matter of "taking a trip," it is missing that crucial element which mysticism refers to as a process of purification. Traveling along a long spiritual path involves an essential transformation of the person. Such a transformation cannot be achieved in most cases in a drug experience. Often these are only pseudomystical experiences that remain on the emotional level.

How do we tell the difference between genuine and pseudomystical experience?

Pseudomystical experiences do not lead us to a higher, transpersonal state of the spirit transcending our everyday ego-consciousness. Instead they throw us back to the prepersonal level. There we experience a condition of symbiotic unity, similar to what nursing babies experience at the mother's breast. This type of experience of unity—often very deep and accompanied by strong emotions—always presupposes an "I" that feels good in that state and wishes to reproduce that experience repeatedly. Thus the pseudomysticism of the New Age movement, as opposed to genuine mysticism, does not transform the person; rather, it reinforces an ego-centered condition precisely by offering pleasant "experiences of oneness" that the ego prides itself on. This is an erroneous conclusion, however, because the ego does not disappear in such an experience. The ego will only be rid of itself if it does not regress to the prepersonal level but transcends that stage and enters the transpersonal level, which means it experiences itself as a mere focus of organization and function—without any permanence. Genuine experience leads to a freedom that transcends everything while a pseudomystical movement can lead to addictive behavior where the ego that faded out momentarily always wants to return to that nice feeling of losing itself. Anyone who extols this as a mystical or spiritual way and makes people dependent on such a way is a charlatan, and a dangerous one at that.

Even though a genuine spiritual master does not urge his students to strive again and again for mystical experiences?

Even he will encourage his students to continue along the spiritual path without stopping. But he will remind them that they cannot have such an experience by means of individual effort. He will tell them that such experiences only happen to persons who have let go of the ego that always wants to achieve and experience something.

He will show them that there is a long and difficult way to that point; it's a process of transformation that makes the ego-structures of our psyche transparent. It can lead through phases of disorientation and discouragement, although it eventually brings us to a point where we know we can confidently leave our ego behind and enter a higher level of reality. Anyone who has had such an experience—whether as student or teacher—will not oblige or bind himself or others to anything.

If mystical experience leads to the freedom and tolerance you've described, why do mystics repeatedly come into conflict with religious institutions?

A mystical experience is a foundational experience, and those who have had that experience cannot keep it to themselves. They must articulate it and will do so in a way that is in keeping with their personality. But that is precisely what religious institutions can only accept with great reserve. That's the reason why the Christian churches compelled the mystics to "re-dogmatize" their experiences. Anyone who refused to do so had to be ready to be persecuted as a heretic or even burned at the stake. People like Marguerite Porete, Giordano Bruno, and Miguel de Molinos are examples of mystics who refused to express their experiences in ways that conformed to dogma and who were punished as a result in the worst ways imaginable. You find this pattern in all theistic religions. These religions lay claim to truth revealed directly by God, after which every other type of experience of God becomes heresy.

How does a mystic react when he or she is condemned as a heretic by a religious institution?

A mystically inspired person will not deny that institutions have a helpful, organizing significance. As a rule, he will not seek out-and-out confrontation. Nevertheless, he will—often unintentionally—call these institutions into question *indirectly* since his mystical experience frequently brings him to a transconfessional sphere beyond the often narrow piety of the established confessions.

Which is also—if not an "a-theistic"—then a "trans-theistic" sphere?

Exactly. That's why mystics get into hot water when they attempt to re-dogmatize their experiences. The language of the religion to which they belong does not have the words to express what they have experienced. The dualistic thought patterns of Christianity make it virtually impossible to articulate a mystical experience of unity. And even when mystics attempted, in spite of it all, to verbalize their experiences, it was often answered only with shaking of heads in disbelief and suspicion on the part of theologians.

That's a sobering statement. Do you see any potential inside the Christian churches for a new spiritual awakening?

Institutions always lag behind. Whenever renewal occurred in the churches, it was from the bottom up. I suspect that things will be similar with the spiritual movement we are presently observing. It occurs from the foundation up and eventually makes its way into the ecclesiastical institutions. What we need is a "transformation of religion" (Ken Wilber). This has to do with a new orientation—a *metanoia* toward the mystical dimension. Religions are groups of people seeking answers to the question of the meaning of their lives. Answers have to be reformulated again and again, also in religion. Those reformulations are subject to the changes of time. The old paradigm says: We are beings who have developed spirit but who have strayed from God through error. The new paradigm says: We have never fallen away from God. What we call God extends like a fan in evolution. We are an epiphany of God. It's only that we fail to realize our true identity. We have not fallen away from this primary reality, as the doctrine of "original sin" would have us understand. We have just forgotten that we come from this reality and never could fall out of it. We consider ourselves to be the shore that craves for the ocean while, in actuality, we are the ocean that plays with the shore. In this realization lies the future of our species. A turning point in the history of religion has been initiated.

*You said that renewal starts from the bottom up. The period after the
Second World War witnessed the appearance of new, often small communities in many parts of Europe which strived very consciously for a
spiritual way of life. The best-known example is probably the community of Taizé, which Roger Schutz founded. What do you think of such
communities?*

They are doubtless forerunners of a new departure in spirituality, although not its actual agents. Such communities lead us out of
the traditional thinking paradigm of the churches without making a
clean break with that paradigm. In that sense they play an important, though limited role.

*Taizé attributes considerable importance to a strong emphasis on litur-
gy and singing. Are these also "transitional phenomena"?*

In my view, Taizé is a mystical movement that seeks to free our
religious potential with rituals and more meditative forms of the liturgy. It doesn't expect people to learn teachings or theories that have
nothing to do with their secular everyday lives. Taizé thus appears to
me to be a particularly successful case of a new departure, no less
and no more. Ultimately it remains an intermediate stage. That's why
people often come to me who took their first steps on the spiritual
path in Taizé but then realized that they'd come to a point where
they needed to deepen that experience.

*In history it was mostly the traditional religious orders—you yourself
belong to one—that acted on the forefront of movements for a new spiritual departure, or were its precursor. Is there still spiritual potential in
the monasteries today?*

Religious orders enjoy a certain leeway that diocesan priests or
bishops do not necessarily have. A Benedictine abbey, for example,
has a certain independence. Religious orders are to some extent au-
tonomous organizations. Thus it was possible for many things to
develop in the monasteries that only became fruitful for the entire
Church in the course of time. I imagine this is still the case today.

As such, the monasteries are something like "theological free-trade zones."

Yes, although there are limits to the "trade." Even a religious order has to observe restraint. Nevertheless, I would hope for more courage to engage in lively exchange. The religious orders could act as a field of experimentation within a rather controlled and centralized institution. As mentioned already, impulses for change in the Church have hardly ever come from above. They all had to make it from below.

Even the interest among Christians in the spirituality of the East emerged from within the monasteries.

That's because, due to their mission activities, they were the first to encounter other forms of devotion. They discovered a wealth of basic truths in other religions that agreed with their own faith in many points. The Trappist monk Thomas Merton (1915–1968) discovered Zen Buddhism for himself and many others in the Western world, and Bede Griffiths (1906–1993) was inspired by his Hindu environment. We could mention other examples showing how, in many cases, it was people in religious orders who opened themselves up for other religions and sought dialogue with them.

But these attitudes are evidently the source of embarrassment for the churches. They attempt to appear open-minded, but are actually very cautious and reserved. The "profile" of each church is brought into sharper relief. Although people are ready to engage in interdenominational dialogue and cooperate in the social and ethical area, there still seems to be considerable fear in the institutions of being classified on the same level as the others.

Outwardly, the churches are very open to one another in their pronouncements. Internally, however, they're afraid of losing their "uniqueness." You still hear expressions such as "the valued-added dimension of Christianity," but the institutions are no longer totally convincing in the way they present themselves. The slogan "Jesus yes,

Church no!" indicates an increase in religiosity outside of institutions. It's understandable that a community of believers will fence itself off in times of crisis and attempt to achieve internal unity. But that can easily result in exclusivity. Retreating into one's fortress has never worked in the long run. The churches lack the courage for integration in a changing society, because such integration would transform the churches themselves—and that's frightening.

Do you mean to say the churches won't be able to stop their decline in membership by a return to the particular characteristics of their confession?

I would expect the opposite. Of course, those requiring a doctrinal framework will remain in the Church so they can feel in possession of the certainty of salvation they long for. In fact, the danger of a regression to the level of religious sects was seldom as great as today. People feel overwhelmed by the demands of modern questions and prefer to retreat into fundamentalist positions instead of working productively for the spiritual development of society. People who cannot bring their understanding of themselves and the world into harmony with the teachings of the churches will continue to leave the churches, perhaps in even greater numbers.

But aren't the churches faced with a dilemma here? On the one hand they have to conform to the demands of the times while, on the other hand, they have to preserve their traditions? Is there any way out of this impasse?

For me, religions are models that we use to define our place in the events of the cosmos. When a species has reached the level of the spirit, it needs answers to questions about the meaning of its existence, questions about where it came from and where it is going. When science creates a model, it does so to explain the facts. When new knowledge is obtained, the model is revised. Religions must attempt to do the same. Our ideas of faith were formed when human beings still believed the earth was flat and the stars were holes in the firmament. We can no longer speak about God in the way it was still possible to do in the nineteenth century. There's a need now for answers to basic questions: What is the significance of humankind in the evolutionary processes of the cosmos? Long overdue are new interpretations of original sin, resurrection, and salvation, about the personality and a-personality of God, timelessness, and eternity. But there are other pressing questions requiring answers, particularly in the Catholic Church: What about equal rights for women in the Church? Don't we need a free choice between celibacy and marriage in the priesthood? Other pressing issues include a more positive attitude toward sexuality, democratic structures in the institutions, getting rid of the image of a punishing God, being prepared to take a critical stance toward developments without wanting to stop them at any cost.

In the United States—and to a certain extent in Germany—we're familiar with a Protestant variation of religious conservatism: the evangelical movements such as the Pentecostals, charismatics, pietists—to mention just a few. These communities are a source of annoyance in respect to what we've been discussing, since on the one hand they determine the thinking and lives of their members with almost fundamentalist verve while on the other hand showing a vigor that leaves no doubt that genuine religious experience is present. How do these two aspects come together?

All groups that assures people salvation will remain in vogue. And anyone who feels at home in them should stay, without being criticized for doing so. But even in these groups, what you have are transitional phenomena. Even the members of such communities reach a certain point and leave. No one, for example, can spend his whole life speaking in tongues. To be sure, speaking in tongues is a spiritual practice in which the ego plays a subordinate role. But it is only one possibility, and can easily lead to elitism. As a matter of fact, in the case of these other "charisms" we are dealing with phenomena that belong more properly to the field of parapsychology. They're not limited to Christianity, as adherents of so-called "primitive" religions also speak in tongues. More and more people come to me who want to go beyond such forms of prayer.

But there are also people who do not sense those limits and submit them-selves instead to the mostly rigid morality of their communities or churches. You don't get much of a feeling of a new spiritual departure in that.

It's true that the danger of sectarianism and fundamentalism is always present. In many cases the longing for security in a group is greater than the desire to make a new departure. This leads to the "wall mentality" so typical of such sects: It wants to fend off and keep at bay anything that could endanger the security they've achieved with such effort. This is the opposite of mystical religiosity that has its center in letting go. Sects, on the other hand, often encourage a frenzied clinging to doctrines, moral commandments, group identi-ties, and the like. The more uncertain people are about things, the more they're tempted to believe the promises of security made by the sects and fundamentalists. That explains to some extent the suc-cess they enjoy.

Along with the retreat into fundamentalism there is another develop-ment that points in the other direction. In recent years we've witnessed numerous encounters between members and leaders of large religious denominations. An openness is emerging that was previously unknown. Do you see in that signs of evolutionary progress toward transconfes-sionality?

No. Interdenominational dialogue is important, as is interdenom-inational action in society, or the common search of religions to-ward a global ethic that would be binding for all peoples and na-tions. What I am attempting is something else. True unity of religions—and I do not shrink from saying, "their actual goal"—is found in the experience of what their holy books, rituals, and cere-monies preach about. It is in this experience of the primary reality that religions encounter one another. They are all striving toward the same peak of a single reality. But that experience transcends all confessions.

*Does that mean global ethics and interreligious dialogue are only in-
termediate stages?*

Why speak in terms of "only"? That sounds too negative. As I
said, such interreligious dialogue is of the greatest significance. But
real unity among religions is not found in syncretism, but in the experience of reality. All religions have discovered mystical ways toward this level of experience, and also teach those ways. Mysticism
will grow in significance in the coming centuries. Indeed, I consider
mysticism to be the rescue of theology. The twenty-first century will
be a "metaphysical century," but theology struggles with this. While
science discovers in Eastern esoteric paths corroborative evidence
for its experiences on the frontiers of research, the mystical path has
fallen into obscurity among theologians.

*Have I understood you correctly that true unity among religions is found
in the transconfessional experience?*

Yes and no. In the experience of the Primary Reality, my name
for "the One and the True," there are no longer any religions to be
united, as there is no differentiation in that reality. In that reality we
experience unity with the One. It might take awhile, but it is precisely here that religions will some day encounter one another—at the
peak of truth. Even then, they will continue to use different terminology about this single truth, according to their culture, their religious images, and ideas. Those are the "stained-glass windows" I was
talking about earlier by which they attempt to explain this single truth
on the rational level. But the actual fact is the light. The religions will
no longer separate themselves from one another or fight with one
another. In the end they will realize that they have, and have always
had, the same goal. I consider the interest of many Europeans in the
esoteric paths of Hinduism and Buddhism to be a positive development. It is an initial sign of our growing awareness of a common,
transconfessional core in all confessions.

Assuming for the moment that an increasing number of people will actually discover a transconfessional spirituality as something valuable, what form will religious life assume in the future?

As already mentioned, there will be basic groups on a larger scale that will center around spiritual guides or leaders within their churches and who have recognized that way as valid and as giving meaning to their lives. This will inevitably have an effect on the traditional churches. They will no longer be able to avoid coming to terms with this development, which means including spiritual-mystical elements in their propagation of the faith and in their religious practices to a greater extent than heretofore.

What does that mean in concrete terms?

There seems to be a crying need to attribute greater importance to mysticism and spirituality in the training of theologians. It must be possible for people interested in spiritual matters to find a place or a home in the Church. To that end, it is naturally desirable that those in the Church responsible for teaching no longer display a barely concealed rejection of anything to do with mysticism. In my opinion, the Church only hurts itself when it warns its members about getting involved in contemplation and mysticism.

You said that training of theologians must be reformed. Does that involve the content of what is taught in the disciplines of theology, or do you mean the theologians themselves should practice contemplation?

Both. Primarily it means that those training for pastoral positions in the Church must first come to see that spiritual experiences are a reality. By and large, our theologians are at a total loss when someone comes to them who has broken through to the transpersonal sphere. People who have had a spiritual crisis—or an authentic mystical experience—and seek assistance in sorting out that experience will generally be far more inclined to visit a psychologist, psychotherapist, or nonmedical practitioner than a priest or pastor. A study shows that only about 20 percent of those people seek out assistance

from their church. Clearly, the majority of people do not consider
the churches particularly competent in such matters. This is an alarming
situation.

Would the reputation of the churches and their representatives improve
if they appeared before us with the authority derived from spiritual
experience? I find it indicative of the situation that a figure like the
Dalai Lama can impress so many people, even within the inner circles
of the churches.

We need not call on the services of the Dalai Lama for that purpose—Pope John Paul II was in that respect every bit the Dalai Lama's equal. He gave security and orientation while possessing a charismatic authority. But that alone is not enough. What was missing in
his case are truly religious themes, not to mention openness and tolerance—there was too much talk about moral demands. Be that as it
may, his authority and credibility were no doubt nourished by his
own very personal piety.

CHAPTER 3

God as Dancer and Dance

A New Interpretation
of Christian Doctrines

Let's take a short excursion into the field of Christian theology. You mentioned that theology seems to run into curious difficulties when it comes to mysticism. Why do Christian mysticism and Christian theology have such a hard time with each other?

Mysticism finds its foundation in an experience of unity where separation between God and the world disappears. Christian theology, on the other hand, is founded on a fundamental dualism between God and the world. According to this theistic idea, God is a person existing for himself, outside the world. He has created the world as an existence separate from himself and rules it from outside. The world for its part, as a creation separate from God, has the possibility of behaving in one way or another toward its creator. This responsibility has been placed in the lap of humankind. But we fell from grace through sin, so that the world is a "fallen" world. Since then, the world and God are separate, not only in terms of their existence but also in terms of their quality. The world is in need of salvation; but salvation can only come from outside—from God. God must take the initiative in closing the gap that has opened up between us. And he does so by sending a redeemer and savior to the

51

world, a preexistent savior equal to God, who comes into the world as God, becomes a man, and finally saves humanity through a sacrifice. According to Christian theology, it is the blood of Christ, his death of atonement on the cross that brings about reconciliation between God and the fallen world. To make such a theological interpretation plausible to modern people is becoming increasingly difficult.

Nevertheless, our everyday understanding holds fast to this teaching. Why such tenacity?

It has to do with the structure of the human mind. Today we know that we do not simply apprehend the world neutrally. Our conception of the world is based on the brain's ability to perceive. We know now that there are no colors or sounds outside of us, only frequencies. It is the brain that constructs a particular world from those frequencies, while the brains of whales and porpoises produce a completely different world from that same essence. There is no Archimedean point from which the world can be perceived "as it really is." The perceiver is always involved in the process of perception. If that is true, then we have to ask ourselves how things stand with our abilities of perception. And if we pursue that question we realize that our reason is dualistically structured. We perceive by making distinctions, by creating boundaries. It is "de-fining" in the original sense of creating boundaries. Aristotle says we have knowledge of something and are able to state in what way it differs from an object of the same type. This dualistic structure of our power of perception is transferred to reality. We believe that reality is also dualistically organized, because our reason knows no other method of accessing reality— *our* reason, mind you, because our feelings and mystical experience open us to a totally different experience of reality.

If our reason alienates us in that way from reality, and theology is a rational affair, wouldn't it be better for mysticism to dispense with theology altogether?

Religion stands on two legs: mysticism and theology. Take one away and you remove the other. But we have to realize that theology plays no role in the experience itself. It begins where the experiences leaves off. Issuing from the experience, it should actually lead back to that experience. In my opinion, mysticism can become the liberation of theology. After a mystical experience in the church of Vosa Nova toward the end of his life, Thomas Aquinas said: "All I have written seems to me like straw compared to what I have seen and what has been revealed to me." In other words: From the mystical experience of reality emerges another view of religion, and going hand in hand with that is another form of theology.

What type of religion and theology would that be?

Some clever person once said: "Religion is a trick of our genes." I take this statement very seriously and believe it is not at all in our interests to disqualify religion. On the contrary: When a species has reached a particular level of evolution where it begins to pose questions about where it came from, about its future and its ultimate significance, it's only natural for it to create a capacity that will help it find answers to those questions. The result is religion. It has fulfilled its task outstandingly over the millennia and continues to do so today. Religion is part of evolution. When we come to the present point, where the answers of religion are no longer tenable, it's a sign that evolution has progressed and that a new capacity for self-understanding must appear. Religion develops along with humankind. An "evolutionary theology" wishes to take this situation into account. Such a theology proceeds from an unfolding and development of life. It perceives a continual appearance and disappearance in all things. Mysticism says, "The world is born anew in each moment." It assumes that this ever-new creation is not achieved through the hand of a creator standing outside of evolution. It occurs by itself, following its own impulse. In the view of mystical or evolutionary theology,

God is not the initiator of evolution, acting from outside. Evolution is God unfolding himself.

You say that God is evolution. Is there any sense at all, then, in still speaking about God?

We could hardly dispense with the word. Nevertheless, we should always be clear about how we want it to be understood. In our everyday understanding the word *God* is connected with the traditional theistic idea of power in the form of a person standing outside of creation. Thus, when speaking about what is actually meant by the word *God*, I prefer to speak in terms of the *Primary Reality*. Zen speaks in the term of *Emptiness* and Hinduism in the term of *Brahman*. Meister Eckhart spoke of the *Godhead* and Johannes Tauler (1300–1361) about the *Ultimate Ground*. Whatever the terminology, what is meant in all cases is something we can actually say nothing about. It's a concept without a determinable content, a concept so completely different from other concepts that Eckhart could say: "The difference between God and the Godhead are greater than between heaven and earth."

In your writings you bring the concept of life into close contact with the concept of God.

Life is an apt concept to characterize the reality we call *God*. For life, too, eludes our grasp. We neither know where it comes from nor where it is going. Life is everywhere and nowhere. It reveals itself in every single creature, but it is always more than any individual creature. This is precisely the case with the Primary Reality. It is there, but is only apprehensible in the form it assumes. The reality itself is emptiness, which requires form in order to appear. For without emptiness there could be no form since form is always the form of emptiness. It's exactly the same with life. Life is in every living creature, for without life a creature would not be a creature. But life is never exhausted in any single creature. It is always greater than the individual creature. It comes and goes with the creatures and remains nevertheless ungraspable.

Do I understand you correctly that you not only place life and God in an analogy to each other but also consider them to be two different definitions of the Primary Reality?

Yes, to the extent that we understand by "life" this great, ungraspable energy of the One that pervades all of creation and acts as the driving force. We could also refer to this power as the "Life of God." Or, you can use the definition of the French physicist J. E. Charón (1920–1998) and call it "Love"—not personal love but love in the sense of absolute openness for each and every thing. In that sense, life is actually the structural principle of evolution—the readiness of an atom to bind itself with another atom in the form of a molecule. It is the readiness of molecules to jointly create a cell, the readiness of cells to become a greater organism. This readiness for self-transcendence can be recognized throughout the cosmos. It is no other than the driving force of life and evolution. Only those who can maintain their identity while simultaneously transcending themselves have a chance of survival in the process of evolution.

The classical theory of evolution, however, teaches us that it is not love that is the driving motor of evolution but the principle of "survival of the fittest."

That is not necessarily always the case. Today we know it is not only brute strength but also the ability to adapt and cooperate. It was not always the animal with the largest teeth or the most poisonous stinger that prevailed, it was also the biotopes—living systems that harmonize perfectly with one another and simultaneously have the ability to open themselves and transcend themselves. Systems, on the other hand, that are closed in upon themselves perish, as we can see in the case of cancerous growths or incestuous families.

God, life, love, evolution—four names for the same reality?

Yes. God cannot be separated from evolution. God is coming and going. God is being born and dying. God is the dancer who dances the dance of evolution. A dancer without a dance makes no sense—

anymore than a dance without a dancer. In this way, God and evolution belong together. The one is unthinkable without the other. Or take the example of a symphony. The cosmos is a symphony and what we refer to as "God" sounds as this symphony. Each place, each moment, each creation, is a particular note, indispensable for the whole, even when it makes way for another note in the next instant. All the notes create the whole, all notes *are* the whole—and that which creates the wholeness of the whole is God, which sounds as this totality.

That sounds a little like a subtle new interpretation of the Christian idea of the Incarnation: God incarnated as a cosmic symphony.

God incarnates in the cosmos. He and his incarnations are inseparably connected with one another. He is not *in* his incarnation: He manifests himself *as* incarnation. He reveals himself in the tree as tree, in the animal as animal, in the person as person, and in the angel as angel. They are not creatures in addition to which there is a God who slips into them. God is each and every one of these creatures and yet he is not them, since God never exhausts himself in any single creature but is always all the others as well. It is precisely this that is the experience of the mystic. The mystic apprehends the cosmos as the meaningful manifestation of God, while many people behave toward the cosmos like illiterates toward a poem. They count the individual letters and words but are unable to understand the meaning that gives the entire poem its form.

If the cosmos is the manifestation of God that would mean the idea of the Bible as a unique witness to divine revelation is obsolete.

It is not the historical content of any holy books—whether the Bible, the Koran, or the Upanishads—that is of significance. It is their "quality of salvation," and that aspect transcends the purely historical dimension. If interest in the historical interpretation becomes too important, this "quality of salvation" is lost. The New Testament, for example, is not simply composed of the gospels. There are many authors, each of whom has brought a unique understanding of salvation and pronouncements thereof to the writing. It is these statements that are decisive—regardless of whether they are the work of Paul or the author of the Gospel of John. Revelation comes from the mystical experience of God. It is only then that it is put into words. Holy writings are interpretations of mystical experience. For me the Gospel of John and the apocryphal Gospel of Thomas are as important as the Gospel of Luke. They show us how varied and diverse Christian faith once was before it was forced into the strictures of a system.

How, in your opinion, should we read the Bible?

Like any other sacred writing, the Bible allows for a number of different ways of reading. You can read it in a fundamentalist manner, in terms of its moral message, from a psychological perspective, or from the spiritual level, that is, in terms of its message of salvation. The original Christian communities evidently also read it in that way. That is why we already have differing theologies in various New Testament communities. And that number increases exponentially if we include the apocryphal gospels.

Is this last-mentioned method of reading the Bible the one you yourself prefer?

I do not find it especially useful, at any rate, to put an excessive amount of scholarly astuteness into answering historical questions. It is the message of salvation that is important. People reading the Upanishads do not ask whether the contents are true or who wrote them. Salvation is proclaimed in those writings on very different levels.

What approach should we take to the stories of Jesus' miracles?

I think it is probable that Jesus was also a healer, although his significance is naturally not exhausted in that single aspect. Throughout human history there have been people who were able to employ energies and powers to achieve healing. As the example of faith healing shows, there are also healers in our own times who can activate through their hands the healing energies lying dormant in other people. Actually, though, it's not important whether Jesus was such a person or not. His significance lies on a much more profound level.

What is your opinion of the Christian doctrine, described earlier, according to which Jesus is the Son of God who died a death of atonement on the cross for the salvation of all people?

I do not have any difficulties in referring to Jesus as the Son of God. For me there is nothing that couldn't be the Son of God. The "Son of God" is a description of all people and all creatures. God has incarnated himself in everything that has form. We refer to ourselves as children of God. The peculiarity of Jesus is found in his experience of unity with that which he referred to as Father, out of which he lived and acted. In that sense he is unique.

And what about the doctrine of a death of atonement on the cross?

Jesus himself did not understand his death as a redeeming death. It's actually quite difficult to make this doctrine understandable for people of today. They can no longer find meaning in all the metaphors of blood and atonement. One reason is that we now know where this terminology comes from. The references that the New Testament authors make back to the Old Testament reveal that this language has its roots in an ancient rite where a priest placed the transgressions of an entire community on a ram (thus our term *scapegoat*), after which the ram was butchered and the people were sprayed with its "atoning blood." A second ram was driven into the desert together with the sins of the community in order to appease the spirits dwelling there. (See the Book of Leviticus, chapter 8.) Such mythology requires a contemporary interpretation for modern people. Attempts have also been made in that direction, although none of them have satisfied me up to now.

What is the other aspect you were mentioning?

The second aspect is that modern people are no longer able to accept the claim to exclusive validity as found in Christian theology. Modern people cannot and will not believe that the death of Jesus has a cosmic, all-embracing dimension for all living things. They come into contact with other religions and see the seriousness and moral demands with which their adherents proceed along their own paths to salvation. They consider it implausible that all this should have been reduced to empty gesturing through the death of a single person two thousand years ago. May I remind you about the 125 billion galaxies in our universe and the nearly *fourteen* billion years that our cosmos is supposed to have been in existence already? In what context can we today place the appearance of Jesus and his life? This, in my opinion, raises very serious questions for theology.

But theologians have been posing this question for a long time now already. At any rate, it is only a small minority of biblical exegetes who claim that Jesus understood his death as a death of atonement.

It's true that the majority of theologians shy away from supporting the doctrine of the sacrificial or expiatory death of Jesus. Nevertheless, it is securely anchored in the foundation of Christian faith. Just consider the Holy Week liturgy in all the liturgical traditions. Of course, you can say that theological doctrine and what is actually preached in the various communities diverge considerably from one another, but this discrepancy is precisely what puts an immense strain on Christianity today as it fails to provide a Christology that can be broadly reliable, that is, a teaching that provides every believing person with understandable information on how the influence and death of Jesus of Nazareth can be understood.

But today we witness wide-ranging research on Jesus.

Certainly, and it provides us with information about Jesus at a heretofore unknown level. We know more about him than people of the second century did, if not people in the final decades of the first

Christian century. But the results of research on Jesus are unable to resolve the inner contradictions in our picture of Christ. To the contrary, they provide more fuel for the fire in rejecting the conventional model of expiatory death on the cross, thus increasing the tension regarding the basic dualistic-theistic structure of Christian theology. Research on the life of Jesus teaches us that Jesus was a man, a teacher of salvation and wandering preacher who—as was common in his times—gathered disciples around him and came with his teachings into conflict with the established religious and political institutions, with the result that he had to die. According to this view, Jesus did not die an expiatory death, but the death of a prophet, as had many other spiritual teachers of Israel before him. There is agreement among many theologians regarding this other image of Jesus. But no one dares to venture a bolder interpretation of the facts. I am not satisfied with what I've read on the subject.

What significance remains for the entire tradition about Jesus if the conventional interpretation is inaccurate?

As I said previously, its meaning is not found in its historical or doctrinal content, but solely in its message of salvation.

Could you explain to us by way of an example what is the "message of salvation" of a biblical story?

Take for example the story of what happened on Mount Tabor, which is told in the ninth chapter of the Gospel of Mark. Jesus is transfigured before the eyes of his disciples. Suddenly they realize that Jesus is someone completely different from whom they had believed him to be until then. They become aware of his divinity and recognize him as the Son of God. The salvation message in this story is found in the fact that it not only deals with the revelation of the true form of Jesus but also says something about the true form of every person, indeed, of every existence. *We* are what is meant here. Jesus is the type by which God wants to make the mystery of his incarnation visible in us.

But what about the preaching of Jesus?

He himself is his own preaching or propagation. What is it, after all, that he proclaims in his preaching? It is the reign of God: The reign of God is at hand, it is here, it is in us. If we would take seriously the message of salvation found in this preaching, we would no longer have to shrink away from using words like the following in speaking about ourselves: childhood of God, the reign of God in us, "And whoever sees me sees him who sent me" (John 12:45), and "…before Abraham was, I am" (John 8:58). In my opinion, this central element of Jesus' message is recognizable in a story which, although not specifically Christian, is also told by Jesus in a particular variation. It is the story of the prodigal son. It deals with a young man who asks for his inheritance and then throws himself blindly into life. One day he realizes that this life can't be the real life. He asks about the meaning of life and realizes that he must return to his father, back to his true essence. It is only there that he can find what he is looking for. Only there can he find his true home. His father is waiting for him. There are no reproaches; there is no wagging of a reproving finger. Give him shoes, a decent set of clothes, and a ring on his finger. Let us celebrate. He has realized his divine essence, he knows who he is. In this story and others, Jesus shows us the way to salvation. This parable is a guide along our way in life. It can help us to orient ourselves by telling us who we really are: sons and daughters, inheritors of the reign of God. Unfortunately, theologians have all too often given the story a moralistic slant: The son turns his back on God and lives in sin. He realizes his error, does penance, and is finally welcomed back in grace by his merciful father. You can see the difference. The conventional way of understanding the story is based on the idea of a personal God in heaven somewhere. The other interpretation puts the emphasis on telling people how they can awaken to their real life under the guidance of Jesus.

The story of the prodigal son is a parable of Jesus with a clearly didactic purpose. But, as to the stories in the New Testament about Jesus' life and deeds, can one find a similar message of salvation there?

A good example is the story of the birth of Jesus. Those who busy themselves with asking whether everything really occurred as related in the Gospel of Luke will miss the actual meaning of the story. We come closer to that meaning when we take the time to compare the story with the written traditions of other religions. We notice, for example, that there is an almost identical story regarding the birth of Krishna. There, too, you read about an "immaculate conception" and virgin birth. Also, in that story there is a bad person who hunts for the newborn baby, seeking to kill him. Even the shepherds in the fields aren't missing! In short, there are grounds for believing that the Christian story of Christmas was adapted from the story of the birth of Krishna. The only people who will find this problematic are those keen on establishing the historical veracity of the story. Those, on the other hand, who pose the question about its meaning in terms of salvation will tend to see in this agreement between the two stories a sign of the actual truth revealed in the story. The story is about us. It concerns our birth from God. Jesus and Krishna are each in their own way archetypes of the person born from God and bound in unity with God.

Catholics celebrate the feast of the Immaculate Conception. Scientifically informed persons react with incomprehension to this teaching. A good many have even left the Church as a result.

Whatever others may understand in this teaching, for me the feast of the Immaculate Conception is the celebration of our own divine essence. This feast does not only concern Mary. All of us have been conceived immaculately. In this feast we celebrate our own immaculate conception from God. Meister Eckhart points to our origin in God in one of his sermons:

...for the Father begets his Son in the soul exactly as he does in eternity and not otherwise. He must do so whether he will or not. The Father ceaselessly begets his Son and, what is more, he begets me not only as his Son but as himself and himself as myself, begetting me in his own nature, his own being. At that inmost Source, I spring from the Holy Spirit and there is one life, one being, one action. All God's works are one and therefore He begets me as he does his Son and without distinction.[1]

All well and good, but why does this "birth of God" have to be preceded by an immaculate conception? Or to pose the question differently: Where do you see a salvation message in being conceived without sin?

In every living thing there is something that is not touched by any guilt, where we have never done anything wrong. There we encounter the "unprofaned face" of the person, as Gertrud von le Fort (1876–1971) expresses it. There is our "true face before our birth," as Zen puts it. There we find neither the evil of the world nor guilt. The pronouncement of the Immaculate Conception wishes to show us that our deepest essence is divine. This primal divine principle has created itself as this human form, as Jesus, as Mary, and as this form of mine. It has limited itself in this form and in all forms of a physical, psychological, or spiritual nature. This incorruptible primal principle, which we refer to as God, lives as these forms. It cannot be stained or sullied. It shows itself with shining clarity in our suffering and indeed in our very failings. This true nature means cheerfulness, joy, and serenity. There I am certain that nothing can happen to me in life. Neither criticism nor praise reaches me, neither disgrace nor disaster. All petty self-seeking has disappeared. A great love flows through me. It might sound like I'm getting carried away, but that is true life.

Are there comparable ideas in other religions?

Yes, indeed. Perhaps it's not a coincidence that the Buddhists celebrate the Buddha's enlightenment on the same day that we celebrate the feast of the Immaculate Conception. (Incidentally, it's related about the Buddha as well that his mother was a virgin in conceiving and giving birth to him!) The experience that he had on that day as the morning star twinkled in the sky was exactly the same: "Everything embodies essential nature from the very beginning." That means that all creatures are a manifestation of the same single primal principle that we Europeans refer to as God. You could translate this as meaning that all creatures are conceived without sin. This divine principle has been confirmed for us in baptism. Just as a voice could be heard over Jesus, saying, "This is my beloved Son," this voice is heard over each child that is baptized: This is my beloved son, this is my beloved daughter. Baptism confirms that we are children of God, that we are of divine origin, that we have been conceived without sin and that God is truly our father. Baptism does not bring us anything new; it simply reaffirms our divine essence. Or, as expressed in Christian terms: We are divine life having this human experience. We are divine life that has incarnated itself, that has become human. That is the message of the incarnation of God in Jesus. As in Jesus, this divine principle has become human in every one of us. God creates himself in every moment. He creates himself in every creature. Why limit that message to Jesus and Mary?

If I understand you correctly, this birth from God is not an event that happens at a particular point in time; it happens at all times and everywhere.

The most important element of any mystical experience is timelessness. In the Primary Reality there is no time. Time is not a reality existing for itself; it is a product of our reason that cannot help but think in terms of past, present, and future. For this reason, the presence of God—the birth of God in the person—cannot be realized under chronological criteria. It occurs beyond time; and when it occurs in experience, time ceases to exist.

If it is true that there is no time, then the question arises: What sense is there in speaking in terms of a future resurrection of the dead and a life in the next world?

The "next world," or the world hereafter, is not something that will come in the course of time. It is a world beyond time; it is time-lessness. Once we have become clear on that point, we cannot help but modify our ideas of resurrection and life after death. For now it appears that resurrection does not occur at another time in another place, but rather here and now. God occurs as the here-and-now. Religion doesn't mean service to an otherworldly God in heaven while looking out of the corner of one's eye at a possible future reward in heaven. It is the consummation or fulfillment of the here-and-now. It is the consummation of God in our concrete, everyday lives.

But that would mean discarding the idea of the Last Judgment.

Yes, and good riddance! The idea of a divine judge of the world determining at the end of time whether someone deserves salvation or not—or in the vernacular, whether he should go to heaven or hell—has done a great deal of damage and continues to do so. Even when this model is no longer preached in such a crude form from the pulpit, it lives on in the liturgy and popular piety. Thus the idea of a punishing and judging God is deeply rooted in people's psyches. But they are just as incapable of bringing such an idea into agreement with their rational view of the world as the image of the sacrificial lamb. That's hardly surprising, since it's actually a very curious notion that someone is sitting somewhere beyond the world observing it, and who will judge unerringly and omnisciently the deeds of every single person at the end of time.

In the mystical sense, then, heaven and hell are not realities in a world beyond that we will enter after death. They are metaphors for a fulfilled or unfulfilled life in the here-and-now?

That's right. And if it is explained to people in that way, they can gain meaning from these old concepts. But if you're going to insist that earthly existence is a "valley of tears" and that our true life is only to be found in a world beyond—as a reward for a life lived according to the standard norms—you will only merit disbelief, and rightly so. These are mythical images that only regain their relevance in an interpretation for our times.

Do you mean that Christianity should liberate itself from these images?

Many people are conditioned by the image of a punishing God at the end of time and spend their lives in fear and trembling, even when they should know better. A participant in one of my courses (who could stand for many others) told me recently that she had thrown this God out the window quite a few times already. Nothing worked. God came back again to haunt her. She is thinking now of not sending her children to religion class, out of fears that they could be instilled with the same scary images of a punishing God.

But don't we need the idea of a final judgment to motivate the faithful to the moral behavior required of them?

Bringing religion and morality into close company with each other has not been good for religion. Religion basically has nothing to do with morality. Moral integrity and good actions come as a direct consequence of a mystical experience of reality. When threats of hellfire fill that place, moral behavior is no longer something that develops freely from inside, but rather something forced on us from the outside. Yet it is precisely in this exterior world that salvation is promised to us as long as we keep the commandments. Here you can see how much Christian morality is bolstered by the dualistic idea of God as something otherworldly and the idea that people of this world must keep the commandments of an externalized God to find redemption in another future world. Mysticism, on the other hand, says: We can encounter God in the world and when that happens, moral behavior will emerge naturally.

But not all of us are mystics and, as such, commandments and norms would appear indispensable. When you get down to it, doesn't mysticism seem to speak in favor of moral relativism?

Mysticism, with its denial of a dualistic view of humankind and the world, does indeed expect us to believe that everything we refer to as "evil" is part of a single and undivided primary reality. Our understanding bristles against such an idea. Rationally, we cannot accept that suffering, pain, and death are of divine origin, and so we explain "evil" as a deficit in the person. It is a result of insufficient knowledge. I've found no satisfactory answer in theology to the question of evil. Can we really blame everything on human failure?

Are you saying there's no sense in talking about "evil"?

No, I mean that we cannot solve the mystery of evil by relying on reason. To understand evil you have to go to another level, where you experience how suffering and pain are part of the evolutionary happening of God. But you can't convince anyone of this with logical arguments. It is closed to our ordinary understanding. Our reason would have created a very different world, a much better world, a world without sin, suffering, and death. Like it or not, we end up accusing God of botching up things!

How is "evil" depicted in mysticism?

In mystical experience, what we refer to as "evil" cannot be separated from the divine reality. People who were victims of violence have described to me a state of peace and acceptance in such a situation. There is no longer any blame, no fear, and no judging, just the overwhelming certainty that even what we refer to as "sin" belongs without doubt to the divine fulfillment of life. One can have the same experience in a mystical vision. Another quote from Meister Eckhart might be helpful in making this clearer: "Likewise: In every work, even in evil work, in the evil of punishment as much as in the evil of guilt, God's glory reveals itself and shines." Meister Eckhart was attacked roundly for this statement. Small wonder, since these words will evoke opposition as long as we fail to see them on the level on which they were experienced.

Are suffering, fear, and pain phenomena that are only present as long as there is a separate ego that experiences them as such?

That's right. We always call anything that does harm to our ego "evil." If the ego loses importance—as in the experiences just described—then evil will also take on a different significance. To use an image: If a branch only understands itself as branch, then it fears becoming withered and falling away. It sees this process as evil. However, if the branch could see its identity not in its being a branch but in its being the tree, it would lose its fear of falling away, since the tree, the life of the tree, is its true life. That which it actually is goes on living.

Would you say that even fear of death is the result of our worries about the continuance of our ego?

Exactly, and this is where the promise of salvation in the religions is grounded. They promise that this ego will live on in one way or another. Take away this promise of salvation, and you deprive them of their most essential component. Mysticism, on the other hand, frees us from any desire to have the ego live on, since it allows us already while living to experience how our true identity is not found in the ego with which we continue to falsely identify ourselves.

Heaven and hell, resurrection and purgatory—are these all ideas without content from the mystical viewpoint?

They're not without meaning, although we shouldn't attempt to find their meaning in an overly literal understanding of them. Take the example of purgatory. I see here a metaphor for the mystical path, a way of purification of our ego-fixation. This purification—an aspect that all wisdom teachers speak about—is not something that occurs in an imaginary place after death. It happens here and now, not as a punishment but as a realization growing in breadth and scope. It's not because a judging God wants to see our souls purified in purgatory that this process takes place. It's because we are called to growth and liberation in life. But it's a painful way because we continue to identify with a considerable amount of blockage and conditioning of our psyche, even when that is burdensome. Therefore, the way to salvation is not always a primrose path. It leads through sickness, suffering, and deprivation. It's no coincidence that John of the Cross refers to it as the "dark night."

That's another example of how things that appear to be negative in the light of our everyday consciousness can be positive from the mystical standpoint.

I always encourage people in a spiritual crisis to see it as an opportunity and not to misunderstand the suffering they experience as "penance" or punishment for their sins, but as a way to healing and redemption. Although this other fundamental attitude is not so easy to understand, it seems to me to offer a perspective from which suffering and death take on meaning.

Does that mean even what we generally understand as sin or failing is not something we need to fear from the viewpoint of mysticism?

That's a difficult question. Of course, even from the mystical viewpoint there are actions and behaviors that go against life and its development. Yet they shouldn't be criticized because they offend ethical norms, but because they hinder the unfolding and development of life. From a mystical standpoint sin is basically nothing more than refusing self-transcendence, the refusal to open oneself up in love. To put it in another way, the basic structure of sin is fixation on our ego. This can take various concrete forms in our lives: jealousy, hatred, violence, and war.

Why is the refusal of self-transcendence so problematical?

Because it goes against the basic principle of life, that is, against the basic principle of divine evolution. Evolution, which for me is nothing more than an unfolding of the divine principle, calls on creatures to transcend themselves. If a creature refuses to do so, it dedicates itself to its own destruction. Perhaps this is precisely what humanity is doing at present: we're stuck in the evolutionary process because of our egocentricity and withdraw. The cosmos got along without us for more than *thirteen* billion years! If humankind were to disappear from the earth, it would only be going the way of 99 percent of the creatures that once existed here and which have since become extinct.

In that sense, the mystical experience would be the surest way out of such structural sin.

If you understand "sin" not in a moralistic sense but as the egocentric tendency in us all, which is not in conformity with the divine process of evolution, then sin takes on another meaning. In a future stage of evolution, this knowledge will be available to an increasing number of people compared to our present epoch of dualistic and egocentric rationalism. Our current epoch is nearing its end, and there are reasons for believing that dualistic thinking will increasingly recede into the background in the process of evolutionary progress, making room for a mystical experience of our true essence.

If mystical experience takes the place of ethics and morality, it would seem that our relationship to other people would play only a secondary role in the process.

That is a misunderstanding. In experiencing our true essence, we also experience our interconnectedness with all other creatures. When we then turn our attention to the deprived of the world, we no longer do so because ethical norms and commandments tell us to. It's because of our basic experience of interconnectedness with one another. As long as we fail to overcome our ego-fixation as human beings, we will still need commandments. Once we have experienced the unity and interconnectedness of all things, love is no longer the subject of a commandment, but the natural expression of our own essence. It will no longer appear as an action required of us, but as the way of being of transpersonal existence. I'm aware that this might sound a bit pie-in-the-sky for some people. Nevertheless, coexistence worthy of our humanity will remain impossible as long as we fail to experience this reality.

Then paradise would be a world inhabited only by mystics infused with love?

No. Even people who have had a mystical experience must decide for or against particular actions. This freedom of choice will remain and will always cause tensions and differences of opinion. What's more, the laws of evolution will prevail, even when people agree to them on the basis of mystical experience. The lion will not eat straw and the child will not play with the viper. More likely the lion will continue to eat the lamb. The struggle for survival in evolution will not suddenly end, even for us humans. Like it or not, evolution is a matter of eating or being eaten. There will still be earthquakes that will sweep away thousands. Galaxies will be born while others disappear. The evolution of the divine principle has its own rules of behavior that we will never fully understand on the purely mental level. It is not rationally organized, but rather transrationally or a-rationally. We can nevertheless experience how its rules are the rules of an all-embracing life in which we also participate.

It would seem that the classical theological question of theodicy (explaining God's goodness in the presence of evil) has become redundant.

A theology of evolution will not have to ask many of the questions posed in traditional theology. But that doesn't mean fatalism will take over theology. On the contrary, if we understand ourselves and the entire cosmic process as manifestations of divine life, then we are called to participate in that life.

Thus is it meaningful, indeed imperative, to urge people to make great-er efforts along a spiritual path that leads to this mystical experience of unity?

We've been born as human beings to realize who we are and to experience how we participate in the divine. This is what I see as the meaning of life. We are here to become true human beings, to go beyond our individual egos, and to realize that our true essence is the essence of God. When I say this, I am saying it to people who probably have not had a mystical experience themselves. But I still want to say it to encourage them to believe in the possibility of such an experience and to live their lives in such a way that a mystical experience will be possible for them. For this purpose, it is indis-pensable to offer them something that they can understand on the intellectual level and in which they can understand themselves. I have to provide them with something they can trust. I thus have the fol-lowing words of encouragement for people who come to me with their questions about the meaning of life: "Give yourself over to this process of life and trust that it is God's process!" In traditional reli-gious language that means to obey the will of God, not with gnash-ing of teeth but with a basic, unreserved trust that life has meaning. To bring people closer to this trust, teaching them how to let go, how to open themselves, seems to be the most important task a spiritual teacher can take upon himself or herself.

You say that even an intellectually satisfying representation of mystical spirituality has importance in bringing people to the point of setting out on a mystical path. Is this also a call to philosophers to concern themselves more with religious questions?

We spoke earlier about the philosophical and theological tradi-tion of the *philosophia perennis*: ever new attempts to put mystical experiences into a conceptual context or give a mystical interpreta-tion of the world. When these mystical components are missing from philosophy, then something like existentialism or the philosophy of Nietzsche will result. Both philosophies are fully understandable for me; it's just that the God they assume to have killed has already been dead for some time now from the standpoint of mystical experience. However, because the dimension of mystical experience is missing from these philosophies, they are unable to see that the death of God, which they propagate, can actually signal the birth of another, all-encompassing understanding of God. The *philosophia perennis* emerges from that experience and, for that reason, it would be desirable for that tradition to be revived again.

Notes

1. *Meister Eckhart: A Modern Translation,* by Raymond Bernard Blakney (New York: Harper and Row, 1941), 181.

CHAPTER 4

"Waiting at the Bottom of the Cup Is God"

How Science Corroborates the Experience of Mystical Spirituality

In one of your books you write: "Every spiritual path should also be accompanied by the results of scientific research." What is your reason for this statement?

I believe that the basic impulse for the future development of the spirit will come from the natural sciences. It's my hunch that we will experience a rebirth of metaphysics where physicists and biologists—not philosophers and theologians—will be the midwives, as it were. These are the people who, in the course of research on the basic principles of science, increasingly come to the limits of thought. They encounter a reality there that they can neither doubt nor understand using the tools of logic or analytical thinking. The German physicist Max Planck (1858–1947), for example, realized one day: "I have become devout because I thought things to their end and could not think any further. All of us stop thinking much too early." And he wasn't the only one who had such an experience. Other scientists—Erwin Schrödinger, Wolfgang Pauli, Albert Einstein—have, in the process of their research, come ever closer to religion—or to mysticism, to be more precise. We have the terse statement from Werner Heisenberg (1901–1976): "The first drink from the cup of science makes you an atheist, but waiting at the bottom of the cup is God."

Still, one can't help noticing that these scientists found few links to Christianity.

That's right. Albert Einstein (1879–1955) hit the nail on the head in explaining the reason for this when he made a distinction between his own piety and that of traditional Christianity:

> You will hardly find one among the profounder sort of scientific minds without a religious feeling of his own....His religious feeling takes the form of rapturous amazement at the harmony of natural law, which reveals an intelligence of such superiority that compared with it, all the scientific thinking and acting of human beings is an utterly insignificant reflection. This feeling...is beyond question closely akin to that which has possessed the religious geniuses of all ages.[1]

Why are scientists interested in religion and mysticism beyond Christianity?

Theoretical physics in the twentieth century came to a point where it distanced itself from ideas that had been maintained for centuries as unquestionable and evident truths. Belief has been shaken in an objective world that runs its course in space and time according to immovable causal laws. We now know that reality is not something we can pin down objectively; it is the product of our own reason. What we refer to as the universe is our own creation. The human brain and nervous system are only programmed for a limited amount of reality. Thus we only perceive a limited spectrum of frequencies in the field of our sensory organs. Above and below this spectrum, however, there is much more than what we are capable of comprehending. In other words, we can only comprehend a small part of reality, and that small part is ordered and structured according to the capacity of our understanding. Our reason provides us with an apparatus to make the world available. But it would be an error to believe that its instruments are parts of an objective world. Immanuel Kant (1724–1804) demonstrated this very beautifully regarding the categories of space and time. Space and time are not objective realities. They are tools for understanding the world. They do not exist in actual reality. The insights of physics into the relativity of time and space confirm this. Also agreeing with this view is the mystical experience of a transpersonal reality where time and space no longer play any role.

But they do play a role in the Christian religion!

The core of Christian theology clings to a medieval worldview: a tightly structured, causal, geocentric world order. The result is an extraordinary discrepancy between the immanent worldview of Christian theology and the prevailing worldview of most people of our times, influenced as the latter are by the natural sciences. Thus theological metaphors—heaven and hell, Creation and the Last Judgment, for example—lose more and more of their expressive power. Although they might have been understandable to earlier generations, today they often appear obsolete. Incidentally, we have a similar situation regarding social metaphors that we use to describe our relationship to God. Whether we speak in terms of a "King" or a "Lord of the Heavenly Hosts" or a "Good Shepherd," these images are the products of an agrarian class society. They're foreign to our democratic self-understanding.

Are the natural sciences in a better position to provide theologically conclusive metaphors?

They are. The modern scientific worldview agrees for the most part with the spiritual experiences of mysticism and is thus much more capable than classical doctrine of arriving at conclusive theological statements. The American Nobel Prize winning scientist, Gary Zukav, a man who has done research in the field of subatomic particles, writes as follows:

If Bohm's physics, or one similar to it should become the main thrust of physics in the future, the dances [he means worldviews] of East and West could blend in exquisite harmony. Do not be surprised if physics curricula of the twenty-first century include classes in meditation.[2]

Do you agree with that?

Yes, because Zukav—although his manner of expression is admittedly somewhat exaggerated—is simply stating that there are forms of understanding that go beyond our logic and reason, thus offering the possibility of opening dimensions of reality still closed to the intellect but open to spiritual experience. Leading scientists have grasped this. They have seen the limitations of a logical-rational approach and discovered mysticism as a chance for a better understanding of the cosmos. As a result of this insight into the complexity of reality and their ability to apprehend this as a central theme, science is now in a position to provide pictures and concepts for mystical spirituality by which it can be articulated and understood. Mysticism needs such images. Even if it lives from experiences that transcend the intellect's ability to understand them, it cannot ignore the existence of the intellect, which makes a justified claim to understanding reality.

Although duly aware that its abilities are never sufficient to do so?

That is how it should be. Enlightened understanding that sees through its own limitations also knows that, in the end, it can do no more than produce structures by which it can make reality accessible. It creates—to use our metaphor again—the stained-glass windows it needs to make visible the light that shines through them. The light itself is only visible in a mystical experience; and the stained-glass windows that make it comprehensible are provided by science. The two complement each other.

That means that mysticism—contrary to popular opinion—is in no way anti-intellectual.

Mysticism has nothing against reason or intellect. On the contrary, many mystics were educated persons for their times. Mysticism only shows us how reality cannot be grasped in its totality with reason alone. Nicholas of Cusa (1401–1464) once described this situation very aptly in a concept. He writes:

> I have found the place where one can find Thee undisguised. It is surrounded by the coincidence of opposites [*coincidentia oppositorum*]. This is the wall of Paradise in which Thou dwellest. Its gate is guarded by the highest spirit of reason. Unless one overcomes it, the entrance will not open. On the other side of the wall of the coincidence of opposites one can see Thee; on this side, never.[3]

This doesn't mean we can't provide meaningful descriptions of reality that also make transrational mystical experience accessible to intellectual reflection. It was regarding precisely this point that he was struggling in his scientific studies. Modern science follows in his footsteps in that respect.

In what way?

Let me explain it with an example from quantum mechanics, a field of science that has come to the groundbreaking insight that there is no matter. The further we investigate the building blocks of matter, the more we realize that matter is nothing more than energy, regarding whose origin we are not in a position to say anything. Thus as early as 1944, in a lecture delivered on "The Essence of Matter," the physicist Max Planck assessed the situation as follows:

So I declare what I found in my research of the atoms: There is in fact no matter. All matter originates and exists only by a force, which the nucleus parts bring to vibrate and holds together the atoms as a tiny sun system. Matter itself doesn't exist. There exists only the invigorating, invisible and immortal spirit as the source of material.[4]

With this, Max Planck confirms that matter is nothing else than dense energy. The physicist David Bohm (1917–1992) came to similar conclusions. He speaks about a quantum potential that penetrates everything as the final authority and which can be equated with an absolute consciousness.

What effect does this insight have on a scientific understanding of the human person?

We used to believe that the body developed spirit in the course of time. Intelligence was seen as a function of the brain and the nervous system. Since then, however, we've come to realize that it's exactly the other way around. "The immaterial spirit operates the brain," says the brain researcher and Nobel Prize winner John Eccles (1903–1997). He has shown that it is our thoughts and our will that activate neuroproteins in the brain, that is, spiritual processes are reproduced materially; they are not, so to speak, functions of biochemical-material processes. When we have a thought, a feeling, or a wish, that energy is transformed as a molecule in the brain. In other words: our intellectual and emotional energy materializes in the form of those neuroproteins. They are simultaneously tiny keys in search of keyholes. When a cell finds its keyhole in another cell, it has received the information it needs. This process doesn't only occur in the brain, it pervades the entire body. Each cell of the body is in communication with other cells. A thinking spirit manifests itself in each cell.

But this precedence of spiritual impulses over biochemical processes is disputed by many researchers. What are the circumstances that speak in favor of the proposition that the spirit rules the body, and not the other way around?

We've gained important insights in the field of immunology. We now know that our immune system is also dependent on our psychological condition. Depending on our emotional state we are more or less able to ward off disease-causing agents. There are studies showing that particular cells of the immune system are attacked as a result of depression and stress. Take the case of high blood pressure, for example. In 90 percent of all cases, medical research can find no other cause for high blood pressure than psychological stimuli. This clearly shows the extent to which feelings, moods, and thoughts are transformed into chemical messages, resulting either in health or illness. That also means we can affect our physical condition through a change in our psychological condition. Anyone with experience in meditation or contemplation knows how much the practice affects the body.

In what way?

Contemplation brings about an organization and harmonization of our inner energies. We produce neuroproteins that influence the body, psyche, and spirit. This often has a more positive effect on our health than medical therapies that only operate on the physical level, which treat the physical symptoms of an illness but often ignore the actual causes found in the spiritual dimension.

Plainly speaking, then, it's erroneous to believe that we are beings composed of spirit and body. We're actually spirit or spiritual energy.

The cellular biologist Rupert Sheldrake (born 1942) proposes the thesis that organisms owe their particular existence to indivisible "morphogenetic" fields. The development of an egg, according to this theory, is not controlled by chemical processes, but by these meta-fields, which we can neither see nor measure. If, for example, the egg of a dragonfly is tied off in the middle, out of the tied-off half comes forth not a part of the organism but the whole dragonfly. If one cuts off a piece of willow and sticks it into the ground, a new willow comes forth. The part can produce a new whole. The whole, as everyone knows, is more than the sum of its parts. The morphogenetic field is not destroyed; it is present in every part. Morphogenetic fields are what Rupert Sheldrake calls the metastructures that ultimately shape living creatures. He writes:

> Morphogenetic fields shape and direct the entire animate and in-animate creation. And although the fields are free of matter and energy, they still have an effect in space and time, and can even be changed over space and time. If a member of a biological species acquires a new behavior, its morphogenetic field will be altered. If it retains its new behavior long enough, the morphic resonance will set up a reciprocal effect among all the members of the whole species. The morphogenetic fields are the actual cause of the order, regularity, and constancy of the universe—but they can also admit wholly new modes and forms of behavior.[5]

Thus we are not primarily physiological and biological creatures, but beings with a fundamentally spiritual structure. But morphogenetic fields are not limited to the organism as a whole. Even molecules and atoms have them, so that a body is composed of various morphogenetic structures. What we call the universe is really nothing more than the comprehensive morphogenetic structure of all existing things.

Within which the individual creatures would only be something like concentrations or crystallizations?

That's right. The relationship of the individual to the whole in the cosmos can be readily compared to a hologram. A hologram is a picture that can be divided repeatedly in its center, but which by means of a laser beam is capable of appearing anew in each individual part. That means the entire picture is latently present in each individual section. If you understand the cosmos as a hologram, you can say that each person and each thing represents a point in that hologram—everything is, in itself, a representation of the whole. But that also means everything that happens to an individual part has an effect on the whole. We encounter ourselves with our consciousness in a continuous connection with every other consciousness in the universe. According to this theory, our consciousness is a mirror image of the consciousness of all humanity, indeed of the entire cosmos. This mutual relationship extends from the simplest atom to the most distant galaxies, from a simple life impulse of a unicellular organism to the most spiritually gifted beings. Everything is pervaded with the single spirit, which communicates with itself in the cosmos.

That insight turns our entire understanding of ourselves upside down.

So it is. The old paradigm said: "We are human beings who have a spiritual experience." The new paradigm says: "We are spiritual beings who have a human experience." The French physicist and Nobel Prize winner J. E. Charón, whom I cited earlier, once said: "On the level of the spirit, we live the life of the universe together with it."[6] And the universe is nothing more than the manifestation of an energy field in which the primary reality represents itself. Consciousness and matter equally make up this stream of energy. For that reason we encounter the entire cosmos in the depths of our being and experience unity with it in the mystical experience. As a human being I am not separated from the cosmos. I am the fulfillment of this stream of energy—the fulfillment of divine life. If we try to translate this into Christian terminology, we might say that we are divine life who has this human experience which has restricted itself in the form of human existence. As was true for Jesus, this divine life has become human in each of us. What we usually call "person" is actually a false person. That person is nothing more than our ego-consciousness which experiences itself as absolute individuality and effectively hides the fact that it has split off from the primal reality of divine life. This foundational reality only becomes accessible when the ego-consciousness transcends itself in spiritual experience and turns into the cosmic consciousness of divine life.

How can we understand this splitting off of the ego from the primal reality? If everything is one, the ego can't separate itself from the stream of divine life.

The relationship between the individual person and divine life can best be explained by resorting to a concept first coined by Arthur Koestler (1905–1983): that of the holon. A *holon* is—and that is the meaning of the Greek word—a whole, a whole that does not exist for itself alone, but is always also a part of a larger whole. An atom, for example, is a part of a molecule; a molecule is a whole created from atoms, but it is simultaneously also a part of a whole cell; and the cell in turn is part of a whole organism. Thus nothing is exclusively a part or exclusively a whole; everything is both part and whole. The holon thus has two tendencies: It must exist both for its totality and for its partiality. It must maintain a relationship to the whole, but also maintain its own identity. Otherwise it disappears. The more it tends only to one side, the more it loses the other side. If a holon cannot or will not maintain both its identity as a part and its integration in the whole, it dies and disintegrates into its parts. The atom has to be "open" for the molecule, the molecule must be "open" for the cell, and so on. The holon only has meaning and continued existence in a more extensive holon.

What does that mean for us humans?

It means that we can only exist as human beings if we do not simply insist on our identity but also fit ourselves into the larger reality of which we are part. Like all other holons, we are called on to transcend ourselves, to go beyond ourselves. J. E. Charón gave the name "finality" to this law. It does not mean the end and conclusion of everything; it is rather the tendency of all existence toward something greater. Charón does not hesitate to call this tendency "love"— love in the sense of the drive toward self-transcendence inherent in all existence. If the capacity for self-transcendence is lacking, there remains only decline and fall. A closed system lacking the ability of self-transcending communication cannot endure. An eloquent example is the cancer cell. It excludes itself from the organism and causes the organism as a result to deteriorate. Seen in this light, self-transcendence is the basic position of the universe. And it is the fundamental drive of evolution.

Of evolution? In what way?

Our understanding of reality would be false if we described it merely as a static interconnection of wholes and parts. The world is not a "creation" of God, which he organized once and for all at the beginning of time. It is actually a living process of evolution. It is held in motion by love—the capacity of existence for self-transcendence. It begins with the opening of the atom to the molecule and extends to the spiritual sphere. Spirit transcends all holons while simultaneously pervading them, that is, holons create ever new organisms until the organism realizes its own spirituality. Humankind is such an organism, but evolution will not remain at this stage. It will create new holons in which consciousness evolves in an evermore encompassing way. In the next stage we will no longer understand ourselves primarily as individual persons, but as parts of a single, all-embracing humanity.

Do you mean to say that we humans are actually not individuals but only partial aspects of a greater organism? That idea challenges the very core of Western self-understanding.

That would be a misunderstanding. The theory of the holon is in no way anti-individualistic. It only brings to our attention how individuality is not the single and ultimate reality of humanity. From the perspective of the holon, individuality and personality are seen as instruments on which the primary reality plays and through which it expresses itself. The cosmos is a symphony that depends on its individual existences for its sound. Thus individual personality has great significance, although it's not absolute. The individual is a unique and irreplaceable form for expressing the divine. We find here the unshakable value of the individual. That value is not disputed, either by the theory of the holon or by mystical spirituality. It's only that it is justified in another manner than that of our conventional self-understanding where we identify ourselves with our individuality and thus attribute an improper absoluteness to it. This is what mysticism objects to, saying that it is not in terms of "the ego as absolute" that individuality has value, but as the place where God appears in the world.

In other words, in order to correctly understand ourselves—in our individuality—we have to go beyond ourselves, to transcend ourselves.

Yes, and not only to understand ourselves, but to understand reality as a whole: Becoming a realized person means to overcome our fixation on ego-individuality and open ourselves to the divine reality that we essentially are. It is not that I perceive myself or the world as an individual essence; rather, it is that the world realizes itself in me, in the personal manifestation that I refer to as "me." Understanding is not the appropriation of an objective reality by a subjective individual; understanding is a "coming-to-self-awareness" of the transpersonal reality, the transpersonal consciousness. A genuine understanding of reality thus presupposes a relinquishment of ego-individuality.

To Western ways of thinking, which considers this ego-individuality or subjectivity to be the absolute reality, such an idea is an incredible provocation…and equally so for theology.

Yes, but the discoveries of science support this way of seeing things. Theology shrinks back from it, while continuing to preach the perpetuation of the ego in a world beyond. It thus spoils its chances of offering people to get a hold on religious experience. Christianity needs a totally new interpretation, an interpretation that develops a new theology from the riches of cosmological discoveries in the natural sciences.

Notes

1. Albert Einstein, *The World As I See It* (New York, 1949), 28–29.
2. Gary Zukav, *The Dancing Wu Li Masters: An Overview of the New Physics*, Bantam (New York, 1980), 331.
3. Nicholas of Cusa, *Studienausgabe*, III, 133.
4. Max Planck, in, *Zeitschrift für Erfahrungsheilkunde*, 12/90, 807.
5. Rupert Sheldrake, *Das Schöpherische Universum*, Goldmann TB 14014, Foreword.
6. J.E. Charón, *Der Geist der Materie*, (Hamburg, 1979), 140.

PART TWO

The Spiritual Practice
of Mysticism

CHAPTER 5

Sitting, Breathing, and Becoming Quiet Inside

What Steps Can We Take Along the Spiritual Path?

Today there is a veritable flood of literature on mysticism and spirituality. It was a different situation altogether when you first developed an interest in the subject. How did you find your way to mysticism?

My first "mystical experience" occurred when I was five or six years old. My mother had taken me with her to church where there was perpetual adoration. Many candles were burning on the altar and incense wafted through the air. There were only a few people in the church, among them a number of women praying the rosary in the back pews. Somehow their monotone recitation cast a spell on me. For the first time I experienced that there is a level of experience lying beyond normal understanding. I couldn't make sense of it at the time, of course, but speaking from my present perspective I would say that it was my first religious experience in the transpersonal sphere. That experience was very decisive for me, for from then on it was perfectly clear to me that I wanted to become a priest, although the chances were anything but rosy. Studying for the priesthood cost money, and one of my brothers was already at the university. My family would not have been able to afford sending a second child to the university. I remained optimistic nonetheless, convinced that a solution would be found somewhere. And that's how it turned out. A Benedictine priest became friends with my family. He took me with him to the boarding school at the Abbey of Münsterschwarzach. I was able to spend my first years of high school there.

Was there any other time in your youth when you had similar mystical experiences?

No, my interests at that time were more of a theoretical nature. But after I entered the abbey as a novice, the first thing I did was to rummage through the novitiate library in search of mystical literature. I discovered the works of Teresa of Ávila and John of the Cross, as well as *The Cloud of Unknowing.* I also read the works of Professor Alois Mager, a Benedictine. All these books inspired me, and I attempted the spiritual practices described in them—without a teacher and without outside guidance. Although I never told my spiritual director about all these experiments, it was at this time that I had my first "real" mystical experiences, which brought me beyond the mental sphere. They were much more impressive than anything I had ever known in my practice of prayer. Nevertheless, there were considerable reservations at the monastery about anything to do with the mystical, which meant I kept my spiritual practices pretty much to myself. But that didn't stop me from devoting myself to them with the greatest possible zeal.

Is that also one of the reasons you decided one day to go to Japan to learn about Zen Buddhism?

It took a long time before I had a chance to make contact with other spiritual traditions. In 1972 I met the Japanese Zen master Yamada Kôun Roshi in Munich. It was under his guidance that I participated in a Zen *sesshin* (course) for the first time. A few years later my community founded a new monastery in Japan—in the same town where Yamada Roshi had his little center. Although I was already close to fifty, I applied for a post at that new monastery and actually received permission to go there. Now I could visit Yamada Roshi's center every day from our monastery and also participate in his *sesshins*. When our community later moved to Tokyo, I was allowed to stay on in Kamakura and continue my Zen training. I lived in a Buddhist hermitage for half a year and eventually returned to Europe, having undergone a thorough training in Zen practice lasting twelve years altogether, six of which were spent in Japan.

What sort of training was that?

Basically intensive sitting. "Intensive" means four to eight hours a day, and ten to twelve hours a day in a so-called *sesshin* or intensive week. I also had to finish my koan study, which is encouraged by the school of Zen to which I belong. In 1985, I began teaching Zen in Europe and eleven years later I received full accreditation as a Zen teacher from my own Zen master, Yamada Roshi. Since then, I have been authorized to train Zen teachers myself.

But you didn't just remain in the Zen tradition. After returning to Europe, you consciously turned your attention to the Christian mystical tradition. How did that happen?

Even during my years in Japan I never lost interest in Christian mysticism. I was fascinated to discover that Zen contains the same structural elements as Christian mysticism, that the difficulties along the way and even the experiences were similar to a large extent. I thus returned to Germany with a strong desire to revive Christian mysticism. It was my goal—and remains my goal today—to show that we have a spiritual practice in the Christian tradition which, even though in no way inferior to paths found in other religions, has fallen into obscurity.

What, in your opinion, would account for the contemplative way having become obscure?

It's my guess that the main reason is found in how theology has been turned into a science. This is a process that began in the period of the Enlightenment and which has continued up to the present day. Then there are the fears of the Roman Catholic Church of false teachings and the increasing tendency to centralize everything. Thomas Keating, a Cistercian abbot in the United States, has written an overview of the history of contemplation where he finds the reason for the disappearance of this form of prayer in various events, among them the unfortunate tendency to shorten the Ignatian "Spiritual Exercises" into a method of discursive meditation. There are other factors involved: The debate between the institutional Church and quietism, which overemphasized a passive attitude toward prayer; Jansenism, which taught a form of moral determinism; overemphasis on visions and private revelations; the confusion of the true essence of contemplation with phenomena such as levitation, speaking in tongues, stigmata, visions, and pious bigotry; the misrepresentation of mysticism by equating it with unworldly asceticism; and finally the increasing legalism of the Roman Church.

What effect did these various factors have in the past on Catholic forms of prayer?

To answer your question, I'd like to cite a few sentences written by the English Benedictine abbot Cuthbert Butler (1858–1934), a man who was outstandingly familiar with the situation for spirituality around 1900. He summarizes that situation as follows:

Aside from a few extraordinary vocations, normal prayer for everyone, including contemplative monks and nuns, bishops, priests, and laypeople, was systematic meditation according to a precisely determined method. There were four choices: Either contemplation according to three powers, as set out in the Spiritual Exercises, or according to the method of Saint Alphonsus (a slightly revised form of the Ignatian Exercises), or according to the method that Francis de Sales describes in his "Introducing to the Devout Life," and finally according to the method of Saint Sulpice.[1]

Keating follows up on this quote:

> The final nail driven into the traditional teaching (of contemplation) was the claim that it was presumptuous to attempt contemplative prayer. Novices and seminarians thus received a mutilated view of spiritual life which did not agree with the writings, the tradition, and the normal experience of growth in prayer.[2]

In the meantime you've become acquainted both with Eastern and Western forms of spirituality. What are the specific characteristics of Zen and contemplation—and where do they differ from each other?

Let's look first at their similarities. There is only one primary reality, only one truth, only one summit, to which many paths lead. They who climb the mountain experience what unifies all religions. They realize that all spiritual paths of the religions lead to the same summit. And they notice that they exhibit common basic structures, which are independent of their common goal. Thus almost all spiritual paths recommend that beginners concentrate on a single point to bring our restless and wandering consciousness to stillness. In most cases that focal point is the breath—but it can also be a sound, a word, or a litany. In Christianity we are familiar with the Jesus Prayer, in Zen the koan *Mu* is often used, in Amida Buddhism it is the practice of *nembutsu* or reciting the name of Buddha. Sufis recite the ninety-nine names of Allah, and yogis sing the sacred syllable *Om*. None of this involves thinking about the words or sounds, but rather becoming one with the sounds one is reciting. This is the first basic structure, which is found in almost all spiritual paths, regardless of which religion they come from.

And what is the second basic structure?

The second basic structure is an emptying of consciousness. You try not to cling to anything that appears in the consciousness, which for all intents and purposes is empty. You let everything pass by—like a mirror that reflects everything but doesn't identify with anything. In

Zen this approach is known as *shikantaza* (pure sitting), in the Christian tradition we might refer to it as does *The Cloud of Unknowing*, "An insight into naked existence." John of the Cross gives it the name, "loving attention" or pure attention.

The basic structures of the various spiritual paths are thus identical. Are the differences among religions only those of style?

The differences among the various spiritual paths arise from the cultures they are rooted in. Thus, given how it is common in the Far East to sit on the floor, Zen meditation is also practiced for the most part on the floor. In Europe, on the other hand, the particular way one sits does not play such a decisive role, it being of secondary importance here whether you sit on a chair, on a bench, or on the floor.

Let me be a little more concrete. What can a beginning student of a spiritual discipline expect who signs up for a meditation course under your direction? What happens in such a course?

First of all, the participants are introduced to the practice of sitting. It's left up to them how they wish to sit; but most of them decide to sit on the floor because this is the most comfortable position in the long run, even if the muscles and sinews ache in the beginning. Then they learn what posture to assume when sitting and how to practice: observing the breath, focusing on a word, letting their thoughts go by. Periods of sitting are interrupted by periods of slow walking. There are also personal interviews with the teacher, and lectures.

What is the significance of the lectures and personal interviews?

The lectures introduce the paths of Christian mysticism. We don't speak about mysticism in terms of theory. It's more a matter of presenting the ways that can be practiced in Christian mysticism. This helps participants to realize what they are moving toward and where they are at any given time. That is also the actual goal of my publications: to introduce the practice of the great mystics. I had to find my own way in a painful process. I found descriptions of the mystics, but not of their actual practice. The lectures have the additional goal of motivating students in their practice and helping them through difficult phases. I thus address problems in my lectures which experience has shown me to be particularly frequent among beginners.

What is the purpose of the personal interviews?

The personal interviews with the guide on the spiritual path are helpful in freeing students from various blockages that occur during sitting and which hinder their inner composure. The interviews are also a time to answer questions that occur to students while sitting.

You've addressed the subject of the breath. What should students of Zen or contemplation be particularly aware of regarding the breath?

As much as possible, the breath should simply be observed and not manipulated or influenced in any way. A basically relaxed attitude should accompany the practice at all times. The goal of following the breath is to become one with one's inhalations and exhalations. Becoming one can be explained as follows. At the outset there are two: the observer and that which is observed, myself and my breath. The end goal is for both to fall away so that only the breath remains. But it can be a long way toward reaching that goal.

What does it mean to "be just the breath"?

That's difficult to explain. It means a new state of consciousness in which the breath becomes an opening to a more all-encompassing experience in the transpersonal sphere. It is a state of perfect clarity and wakeful presence. In contemplation we thus speak in terms of "the sacrament of the moment." That's because it's only in the presence of the moment that communication with God is possible; it is only in the here-and-now that reality can be experienced.

You said our thoughts should simply be mirrored during our sitting. They are not thought through. But all of us are accustomed to thinking all the time. Isn't that a possible source of difficulty?

Indeed, that's where the actual difficulty of the practice lies. Almost all of us find it very hard not to let ourselves be distracted from the practice. It is very difficult to stay with something more than three seconds. Our ego continually produces new impulses of thinking, wanting, and feeling. This is perfectly normal, for our entire dynamism of life is found in ego-consciousness. It is creative, it has goals, it is full of intellectual tasks that continually break through to our consciousness and put themselves in the foreground. This can be incredibly frustrating and demoralizing in the beginning. But the situation isn't any different in other, more common forms of practice, such as learning to play a musical instrument. Only through practice can we make progress. Anyone who picks up a violin for the first time will have to struggle for a long time before the first clear tones emerge from the instrument. One day, however, it's no longer you who are playing; the violin plays. It's exactly the same on the spiritual path.

That would mean just sitting once is hardly going to bring anything. How long do students sit in the course of the day and how often should they practice?

In our regular meditation courses there are five blocks of sitting each day, each an hour and a half long. These are further divided into three units of twenty-five minutes each. In the short pauses between sittings we walk slowly around the room, although it's not walking in the usual sense. It's a matter of maintaining a contemplative attitude in motion, thus creating a bridge between practice and everyday life. That's the reason for the hour-long period of working meditation found in every course. The participants become aware that contemplation must return back to everyday life. Our way is not the spiritual equivalent of the hundred-yard dash. It's an entry into a way that should find its completion in everyday life. Over the gate of the main temple of the Soto School of Zen there is a text from the thirteenth century: "Only those interested in the problem of life-and-death should enter. Those who are not totally absorbed in that problem have no reason to pass through this portal." That could be a motto for all spiritual paths. Unless someone is really searching for the meaning of life or for God, and doesn't summon up the necessary seriousness, he or she will give up after the first or second course.

Does that mean that anyone wishing to follow a spiritual path must spend a lot of time practicing?

Yes and no, because there are people who come very quickly and unexpectedly to a spiritual breakthrough. When such people come to us, it's not so much an introduction to spiritual practice they need as an interpretation of what they've experienced. Many of them are so disoriented by their experiences that they're afraid of going crazy. In such cases it is the responsibility of the spiritual guide to determine whether there is an actual danger involved or whether this disorientation is simply the way the ego expresses its fear of losing control in the transpersonal sphere. If there are clear pathological indications, then the person should be told in no uncertain terms that he or she is not suited for such a spiritual practice. In other cases it might be important to suggest that the person undergo therapy in tandem with spiritual practice.

You speak about the fear of going crazy that can suddenly overcome a student of Zen or contemplation. Not only fear, but other feelings can arise in the psyche of the one meditating. What do you recommend to your students in dealing with those feelings and emotions?

It's crucially important to know how to appropriately handle our feelings and psychic traumas. Many people are suffering from psychic wounds from childhood or marriage, although not all of them are aware of it. But when they sit on their meditation cushions those inner wounds and injuries rise to the surface of consciousness with incredible tenacity. Fears and emotions, which we thought we had overcome long ago, appear again with considerable force. Physical phenomena, certain parapsychic abilities such as visions, precognition, telepathy, and the like might be activated. In the worst cases, it can lead to situations like those just described where the spiritual journey must be interrupted or discontinued altogether. But for most people it is enough to learn how to deal with such complexes and lessen their intensity without having to suppress them.

What advice do you give your students in dealing appropriately with the "distractions" just described?

As long as these phenomena do not have to be treated in therapy, my basic advice is: Don't attempt to suppress your thoughts and feelings, but also don't concern yourself with them. Just be aware of them and return to your practice. Things only become harder if you identify with those thoughts and feelings or get bogged down in your resentment, anger, or depression. Then it's harder to become free of them. In a correct approach to practice, emotions and fears are taken by the hand and examined, but neither approved nor negated. We thus gain a certain distance from them. If students succeed in doing so, then problems that have bothered them for decades can often disappear on their own. Of course, these are just some general guidelines. A contemplation course involves much more intensive and individual guidance.

You've spoken for the most part about negative feelings. But positive feelings can also arise during meditation, transporting people into euphoric states. How should students deal with such positive feelings?

Such euphoric states can be even more a hindrance on the spiritual path than negative feelings. The temptation to identify with them and adhere to them is all the greater. Suddenly assuming that they are already quite advanced on the spiritual path, people are much less ready to let go of such feelings. For that very reason, the author of *The Cloud of Unknowing* advises his students to hide from God their longing for God during their practice. The fact that even devotional thoughts and feelings have to be left behind is nevertheless a source of considerable difficulty for many students, given how many of us have been encouraged in earlier instructions on prayer to have such thoughts and feelings. In contemplation, however, they are to be rejected in exactly the same way as profane thoughts and feelings.

Thoughts can be a hindrance on the spiritual path, and so can emotions. But you can't simply advise a student of Zen or contemplation to stop thinking and feeling. Isn't the will also a hindrance on the spiritual path?

The will makes up our ego-structure together with our intellect, memory, and feelings. But the ego-structure must move to the background on the spiritual path if it is to be let go of. Our ego cuts out a piece of reality with which to occupy itself. It can be compared to a single octave on a piano. As long as you plunk away on that single octave, you can't hear the other octaves. The tricky thing about the will is that it is tempted to make the matter of spirituality its own thing. It then becomes the ego's own declared goal to get rid of the ego. At this point, you get involved in a tricky paradox, for the will cannot give itself up. As long as you *want* to make progress along the spiritual path, you won't make any. It is only the person who can let go of the will who makes progress.

And there are particular spiritual practices to support that process of letting go? You've already spoken about forms of meditation in which the names of God are spoken or tones are sung. What should a student of contemplation or Zen give heed to in such practices?

The recitation of God's name helps the student to collect and focus the consciousness, both through the vibrations of the sound as well as the constancy of the recitation. The meaning of the words is not important in this case, anymore than how they are emotionally charged. The important thing is becoming one with the sound. For this reason, students of meditation choose a word or sound that agrees with them and which awakens the desired resonance. In his book, *Eins mit Gott,* Lex Hixon (1942–1995) speaks about the effectiveness of singing "Allah-Hu":

Constant awareness of this mystical tone is the contemplative practice in which Bawa initiates his students. He does
not consider this as a meditation technique such as the repetition of a mantra, but as listening to the resonance of God,
which is always there....You attune yourself day and night to
the Allah-Hu with every breath until your breathing not only
becomes a natural remembrance of Allah, but a conscious
emanation of the divine presence....In every breath, the breath
is the resonance of God. Insight that only the divine exists.
"It is Allah, who must honor Allah." "Only Allah can realize
Allah."[3]

*How about litanies and liturgical forms—the rosary, for example—
whose main focus is found in continuous repetition? In this case it's not
simply attuning oneself to a tone.*

In the final analysis, litanies and the like fulfill the same function
as the one just described. Even in the case of reciting the rosary, it's
not a matter of paying attention to the content of the words. It is a
form of contemplative prayer in which the person reciting sinks into
a religious atmosphere that is more helpful than cognitive understanding of words. The monotone droning is an important part of
the process. It is similar with the chanting of the Divine Office by
monks. Even the Catholic litanies such as the oft repeated "We en-
treat you, hear our prayers" do not require being fully aware of the
meaning of every word. It's more a matter of creating a spiritual opening. Incidentally, combining it with specific bodily movements can
assist the recitation. Recitation of Buddhist sutras in Japan, for example, is sometimes accompanied by particular steps. The Sufis move
their bodies rhythmically to Koran verses. A very similar intention
can be found in our processions and pilgrimages.

But to what extent, if any, is this deeper meaning of processions, pilgrimages, recitation of the rosary, and litanies still present in our consciousness? The outsider, in most cases, can't avoid the impression that something is simply being reeled off or played out, without people being mindful of what they are doing.

There is, of course, the danger that meaningful liturgical forms become fossils, empty shells devoid of meaning. This danger is always present when people fail to receive instructions in what they are supposed to do. For that very reason, recitation of the rosary was not recognized for a long time as a contemplative form of prayer. But I know from my father that he, like many others, had deep religious experiences while reciting the rosary.

Does it make any difference if you recite litanies and the like alone or in a group?

If you pray the rosary in a group, it takes on an increased intensity, which someone reciting alone might not experience in certain circumstances. The same is true for chanting of the Divine Office. This form of prayer finds its effect both in the group as well as in the monotone, even recitation. In both cases it's a matter of group prayers creating an energy field that pervades and supports the individual persons in prayer. You'll remember how, in another connection, we were speaking about morphogenetic fields that have an incredible creative power and effect on reality, even though we can't explain how they are produced. It is just such fields that appear when spiritual practices are conducted in groups. When I come back to Haus St. Benedikt after having been away a few days, I can sense immediately whether a course has taken place in the house or not. If you enter a room where contemplation has taken place, you can feel with your body the energies that have been created over that period.

You mentioned just now that recitation of litanies and prayer recitations can be accompanied by bodily movements. It's a fact that, nowadays—even in the rather austere Protestant churches—there is a growing interest in prayer gestures and sacred dancing. What significance is attributed to such practices in the mystical tradition?

The body is closer than the intellect to an all-embracing level of consciousness. The intellect sets limits; it segments reality into partial aspects with which it occupies itself. The body, on the other hand, can open itself up for the whole. And for this reason it is used in all religions as a vehicle for reaching the transmental sphere of consciousness. I should say in *almost* all religions, because in Christianity we have forgotten this spiritual power of the body. In medieval times the body was still included in prayer. In many books from that time there are instructions on groaning and throwing oneself on the ground. Saint Dominic has bequeathed a number of prayer gestures and postures to us. Later, however, the body was defamed as a hindrance to the spirit that had to be tamed or even mortified through ascetic practices. That was a very unfortunate development, since the body can actually be an enormous help, as long as you find the right way to deal with it. And that is precisely what "bodily prayer" is all about.

What does such prayer involve?

In prayer of this sort, we return to primal gestures of humanity that are probably older than vocal prayer using words. Just like the sounds during recitation, the physical gestures serve as a focal point for collecting and focusing the spirit. I become one with my movement until I can say, "I am this movement or gesture." This can have a strong effect on individuals, especially when they've lacked any real relationship to their bodies up to then, which is often the case, incidentally!

What does such a practice look like in concrete terms?

For example, I can stand in the room with my arms outstretched while remaining silent.

That's all?

That's all. Standing is prayer, when I become one with the standing. The same holds for walking. Our lives are dominated by deeds and achievements. In contemplation, however, you only reach your goal by letting go and letting things be.

But doesn't contemplation become very static then?

We practice contemplative dance in order to also experience contemplation as movement. Actual contemplative dance consists of very simple steps repeated over and over. You give your entire attention to the simple steps. One of the great advantages of dancing is that you notice immediately when your concentration has declined and you are no longer one with what you are doing. In taking a false step, you realize that you are no longer concentrating. Becoming one with the step has the same effect as becoming one with your breath or with a sound.

In other words, in contemplative dance it's not a matter of entering a trancelike state, but rather reaching a higher level of consciousness.

The latter is true. But that doesn't mean you can't enter trancelike states during contemplative dance, although that is not the aim. You actually want to prevent that from happening. Someone should thus explain what is important to the practitioners in guiding that contemplative dance. Instead of dizzy or dopey states, spiritual practices should lead to a clear and wakeful consciousness, a spiritual presence that transcends mere concentration of the reasoning mind.

In Christianity such spiritual dancing is not very much in vogue. How are things in Eastern religions? How is the corporal dimension of spirituality taken into account in those traditions?

Almost all spiritual ways start with the body. In the Eastern ways, the full- or half-lotus sitting posture plays an important role. The head, neck, back, and legs are arranged in a certain way. There are also specific ways of holding the hands, known as *mudras*. Acting as symbolic gestures, they combine an external posture with spiritual ideas. Then there are the *asanas* in yoga: bodily positions that make the practitioner transparent and open. The whirling dance movements of the dervishes and the movements of the Sufis to the mantra Allah-Hu, or the *rak'as* (bows and prostrations), show the significance of the body in mystical prayer. The body is always the starting point. It is also the vessel in which the encounter with the divine reality takes place.

In Zen Buddhism we're familiar with different spiritual practices involving the body. They include the Zen art of archery and Qi-Gong, not to mention various martial arts or Tai-Chi. What spiritual power is found in such practices?

I myself took lessons in the Zen art of archery during my time in Japan. The decisive matter in that discipline is concentration on one's own bodily movements and not on the target. It's mainly a matter of the ritual by which you give yourself over to the practice. The same holds for Qi-Gong or Tai-Chi, which also involve bodily practices that can lead to a higher level of consciousness. A prerequisite, of course, is that they are taught by teachers who themselves see the spiritual dimension as foremost.

You also made brief mention of another form of bodily-oriented spirit-uality: pilgrimages. Such pilgrimages are extremely popular nowadays, both among Catholics and Protestants. Are they an expression of a spiritual need?

I wouldn't exclude that. Even if the many people who have discovered pilgrimages do not reflect on the spiritual dimension, it is very likely that a spiritual need is being given expression. The pilgrim walks because of the walking. He does not walk to reach a goal; he walks for the walking itself. The individual steps become the focus of inner concentration. Even on a very ordinary level, this has a calming effect, as anyone who goes for a walk can attest to. We don't have to add anything to the walking itself. Anyone who can become one with the walking can become one with God. I've heard many credible accounts of people who reached this spiritual level while jogging. And why not? When everything falls away and the jogger becomes one with his steps, his consciousness can open up to a new dimension. Then God walks as a person—in my humanity—over this earth and through this time.

God walks in me?

God accomplishes himself in my walking. It is no longer my walking, but God's walking. God walks with us on the earth. Thus our life becomes a pilgrimage. Thus a Sufi could say: "If you continually come closer to me and do this with full devotion, until you become one with my life, then I am the ear with which you hear, the eye with which you see, the hand with which you hold, the foot with which you walk."

In other words: Even if we are not aware of the spiritual dimension of our actions, we carry out actions that arise from a hidden spiritual need?

Exactly. All of us have an incredible longing for simplicity. The more complicated our daily lives become, the greater that need.

Litanies, prayer gestures, sacral dances, pilgrimages—we've addressed a number of keywords which all have a place that is more on the periphery of the popular church. Would it be advisable for the churches to bring these elements back more strongly into the center of their religious life again?

We're gradually becoming aware that the body is our friend on the spiritual path. It is an instrument in which God reverberates. Without an instrument, no music can reverberate. Strange as it seems, our consciousness plays much more purely on the instrument of the body than on the instrument of reason. Our reasoning often interferes in a distracting way with its own sounds. The man on the street still inwardly resists bringing his religious experience toward the outside and showing it bodily. We are no longer accustomed, as people in medieval times were, to holding our arms up in church, to sighing and prostrating ourselves on the ground. But that doesn't mean things have to remain that way. I'm firmly convinced that a more "incarnate prayer" in the sense of a more bodily-oriented prayer can be integrated in our regular common church services.

But aren't you rather alone with that opinion?

Not a few priests and ministers have accepted this view. Although Vatican II was oriented very strongly toward the cognitive dimension of faith and gave central importance to propagation of the faith, I now notice a growing need for silence in Catholicism. That silence must be "filled" of course; it must be practiced. You have to instruct people on how to deal with silence, in the form of prayer gestures and the like, for example. And we can't start soon enough. That's why I find it extremely encouraging that more and more religion teachers want to practice how to deal with silence in schools. It's been shown that most students react positively when a religion class begins with a period of silence. Evidently the daily overdose of information has awakened a longing for stillness.

But the fact is that the services in the large churches have few spiritual elements, so that people who feel such a spiritual longing are advised to make retreats from time to time into a monastery or to seek out places like Haus St. Benedikt where they can attend contemplation courses and the like. Yet they return to everyday life and notice that this spiritual practice can hardly be maintained in their normal lives. What do you recommend to people in such cases? What would you recommend to a single mother of three children who wants to practice a spiritual path?

I would encourage her to find a quiet time during the day, for example, when the children are in kindergarten or in bed. There must be at least a few minutes each day when she has time for herself. She should use this quiet time, if possible every day at the same time. She should sit down and engage in a simple practice. It is important that the quiet time is already part of the daily routine. When the children are older, she might want to get up a half hour earlier than the rest of the family for contemplation, or sit in meditation when the other family members have gone to bed. The many people living alone in society have it easier in this respect. I'm speaking about singles, older people, and commuters, who can generally organize their time quite well. Be that as it may, the decisive factor is the *regularity* of the practice—that it becomes a matter of course like brushing your teeth in the morning.

In other words, it's good to create little rituals for yourself that give your everyday life a particular form.

Exactly. And that also means creating a place in your house or apartment where you can carry out your spiritual practice. You can spread out a blanket to sit on or place a candle there. The important thing is a particular atmosphere that allows you to come to yourself and concentrate. Even the smallest apartment has room for such a sacred area.

That means even very busy people should be able to dedicate themselves to a spiritual way of life.

That is what experiences teaches us. Parents attending our meditation courses are able to practice an intensive spiritual path in spite of the challenges of everyday life. We place a lot of importance on courses that prepare people for the continuation of contemplation in everyday life.

Notes

1. Cuthbert Butler, "Western Mysticism," quoted in Thomas Keating, *Das Gebet der Sammlung* (Münsterschwarzach, 1995), 44.
2. Ibid., 45.
3. Lex Hixon, *Eins mit Gott* (Droemer Knaur, 1992), 189ff.

CHAPTER 6

Off to Paradise

How Spiritual Experiences
Affect Our Actions

It's often said that a mystical experience transforms the person. Are there certain types of behavior that distinguish mystics from other people?

A person's structure of personality is hardly, if ever, changed by a mystical experience. But that doesn't mean the mystical experience disappears without a trace. The person embarks on a process of transformation from the inside—not through externalized moralistic appeals and "Thou shalts." From our own inner experience we gain a new worldview and new values. Those who have had a mystical experience become more tolerant as an attitude of generosity toward life takes residence in the soul. And precisely because it's not something drummed into us from outside but which grows naturally from inner experience, that generosity will continue to effect our overall behavior. The mystical experience pervades our everyday life. If it does not, the practitioner is stuck somewhere along the spiritual path.

Is it the mystical experience that brings about such an inner transformation or does our life change already when we set out on a spiritual path?

The latter is true. You don't have to have extraordinary experiences to bring this inner transformation to bear.

People often find an increasing capacity for calmness and ease after a mystical experience? What's involved here?

Calmness primarily means the ability to let go and accept other people, situations, and relationships. That ability is there to the extent that a fixation on the ego-structure has receded. The less I'm preoccupied with myself, the more I can allow other people and circumstances to be as they are. I also become more tolerant toward myself. With men that means they are no longer so fixated on careers and success. They realize that life is more than business success and making a lot of money. The quality of life starts to become more important than any pure quantity. They take more time for themselves and develop interests in things they didn't even notice before. They suddenly discover reading, for example.

And what about women?

Some women often describe the change as follows: It starts with the books on their bookshelves, proceeds to their wardrobe and eating habits, and goes on to include their circle of friends. Others relate how seemingly ordinary things take on an unexpected meaning. They suddenly discover a spiritual dimension in cooking or cleaning, for example. They're no longer tiresome chores, but practices though which the spirit can effect focused attention. It doesn't happen because they planned it that way, but because their attitude toward life has been transformed from the inside out.

But isn't such a major change in daily habits a source of problems for many people? I'm thinking particularly of couples where one spouse is experiencing changes that the other cannot understand.

That can indeed lead at times to serious crises. A husband suddenly no longer recognizes his wife. That can lead to feelings of fear or aggression. Men often come to me who are afraid their wives might leave them. Such fears, though understandable, are mostly unfounded. A change in one's attitude toward life doesn't necessarily mean radical changes in one's daily life. The calmness we experience in spiritual practice often makes it easier for us to accept existing situations. Nevertheless, I don't want to rule out the possibility that, due to a spiritual experience, energies can be released that prompt someone to end a relationship that has been internally dead for a long time already. When that happens, however, such a decision—though initially painful—is usually good for the parties involved.

So setting out on a spiritual path doesn't necessarily mean a radical transformation of one's lifestyle?

On the contrary, I advise my students to remain where they are: in the workplace, in the family, in their network of relationships in society. It's there that their experience has to prove itself. I advise young people to finish their studies as planned, according to my motto: Religion is life and life is religion. In more exaggerated terms, I could say that when I experience getting up in the morning and putting on my slippers as a deeply religious action, I've realized what religion is. But perhaps that isn't possible without a deep experience.

In other words, mystics aren't necessarily social dropouts.

The *true* mystic, at any rate, is no dropout thumbing his nose at the base world. It's more a matter of encountering God in the world. Meister Eckhart says in this connection: "It is not to be learned by world-flight, running away from things, turning solitary and going apart from the world. Rather, one must learn an inner solitude, wherever or with whomsoever he may be. He must learn to penetrate things and find God there."

The life of a hermit, you would then say, is not very becoming of a mystic.

There *are* people who are called to a life of solitude. But such a lifestyle is the exception. It is based on inner experience and on an inner conviction that, by living that way, we can create an energy field having a positive effect on society. Questions of lifestyle aside, I consider it important and helpful for those seriously desiring to follow a spiritual path to withdraw from everyday life from time to time, although it should always lead back into everyday life. Our task as people is to be people. If there is anything God wants to do with us as persons, it is to be manifested in us as persons. That doesn't mean making a show of retiring from society. On the contrary: Those who make an external retreat from life in a show of asceticism can be easily lulled into believing that they have also achieved an internal retreat. But there's no guarantee for that.

How about monastic forms of life? Most Christian monasteries have made a conscious attempt to retreat to the edge of society in the conviction that they are practicing an especially apt form of religious life.

That is correct in one sense, yet we have to realize that only very few monasteries really retire fully from the world. Most of them have been actively involved in social change, exerting considerable influence on their surroundings. Our own abbey at Münsterschwarzach employs two hundred fifty people in its administrative activities. As this example shows, monasteries are not hermitages—except perhaps in cases like the Carmelite nuns.

The monastic virtues include humility. Does the idea of humility have any significance in the field of mysticism?

Very much so. The Latin word for humility is *humilitas*. Like the word *humanitas*, it comes from the root-word *humus*, which means earth, dirt, or fertilizer. Even our word *humor* comes from this root. This shows us that we should approach ourselves and the world with cheerfulness and serenity, with a smile. We shouldn't take ourselves too seriously but maintain our sense of humor, applying ourselves to the way in all humility. What else is humility, after all, than an all-embracing self-acceptance? That doesn't mean I simply resign myself to my weaknesses and faults. Nevertheless I accept that I have received this legacy from life. I don't concentrate excessively on attempting to do away with that legacy or forcing it to do my will. That would amount to remaining stuck in egocentricity.

Mystical experience, we have heard, brings about tolerance, inner calm, and acceptance. But couldn't we also say that mysticism results in a fatalistic attitude of shirking our responsibility toward the world?

You don't climb a mountain to sit forever on the summit. After the ascent comes the descent. Jesus reminded us of this when, following his transfiguration, he refused to allow three houses to be built on the summit as his disciples wanted. Instead he told them to descend from the mountain. Arriving at the foot, he told them he would now go to Jerusalem to undergo his passion and death. What does this tell us? Any mysticism that seeks a permanent escape from the world is pseudomysticism. It is a case of regression; while genuine mystical experience leads us inevitably back into daily life. Mysticism is everyday life; for it is in everyday life that we encounter the primary reality. It is only in that moment of life fully lived that communication with God can occur. Religious art has revealed the symbol of the mandorla to represent this fact.

What does that symbol involve?

The mandorla is formed from two overlapping circles: the circle of human personality and the circle of divine "transpersonality." In art of the Romanesque period, Christ is depicted within the two circles of the mandorla. This is true also for Shakyamuni Buddha in Buddhist art. The mandorla, probably older than either Christianity or Buddhism, characterizes the supernatural and natural, the divine and the human. The place where the circles overlap is "God-Man." It is the region where these two aspects of reality coincide. Mysticism, therefore, is not a matter of departing from the world or of contempt for the world. It is a totally new form of love for the world.

But the question remains: How do mystics return to the world? Do they return with the humility and inner calm we spoke of, or with an inner drive to reform society, as Dorothee Sölle maintains in her book Mystik und Widerstand?

The central focus of the mystical experience is realizing our unity with all living things. That also means experiencing the suffering of others as our own suffering, their joy as our own joy. Upon experiencing that fact, our entire social behavior will change—not because we have arrived at a moral conviction, but because something has changed in us. We have come to an insight that motivates us to charitable works or engagement in society. Rather than "resistance," I prefer the term "social responsibility"—a social responsibility arising from love. This love—the Greek word is *agape*—is an essential component or aspect of mystical experience. Buddhists speak more in terms of compassion, but are essentially referring to the same thing. Armapa has expressed very beautifully in a prayer how compassion arises from mystical experience. He says: "In the moment of enlightenment, in beholding the original face of the Spirit, a boundless compassion arises in me. The greater the enlightenment, the greater the compassion." Regardless of whether we speak in terms of love or compassion, if this feeling fails to possess the soul of the mystic, it is an indication that the experience has been either not genuine or very superficial.

Are you saying that persons who have experienced unity with all living creatures in the mystical experience, and who sense an impulse toward social action from this experience, act correct per se in terms of ethics?

Yes, in one sense. A mystical experience is accompanied by a feeling of boundless mercy and love toward all of creation. It thus reduces any tendency toward immoral or antisocial behavior, for where love has been enkindled there is no longer any room for evil. In this connection I am fond of quoting Saint Augustine: *Ama et fac quod vis,*

"Love and do what you wish!" What he means is, when love is the norm of our actions, we know what we have to do. At the same time, even mystics can go wrong, for we remain conditioned by our culture, religion, childhood experiences, and education. There's no guarantee that we will rid ourselves of those influences. In the last analysis, even mystics have to come to terms with their environment. But we've already achieved quite a lot if we are able to see through this conditioning, although even that doesn't happen all the time!

You've broached a topic that is a source of pain for many people. On the face of it, it wouldn't seem totally unfounded to expect a particularly high level of moral integrity from mystics and spiritual masters. Accordingly, many friends and adherents of Zen Buddhism react with consternation upon hearing that eminent Zen masters gave their unswerving support to Japanese war ideology during the Second World War. You can't help but wonder how something of that sort was possible.

I've been asking myself similar questions, especially since those charges dealt with Yasutani Roshi and Harada Roshi, two teachers from the school of Zen in which I trained. The only explanation I can find for their behavior during the war is the fact that they were raised from childhood in the tradition of the Japanese cult of the emperor. They were conditioned to such a degree by the education they received that it was almost impossible for them to divest themselves of those ideas. They gave credence to intransigent imperialism and outright approval to killing the enemy, to a degree that seems brutal from our perspective. Incidentally, they were able to reconcile their attitudes with the teachings of Zen with no great difficulty. For if everything is simply the molding of the same cosmic life, then the death of an individual hardly makes any difference in the universal process of divine evolution. Evolution proceeds over the slaughter of millions. That is its structural principle.

But you can't justify the deaths of hundreds of thousands of people simply by citing the cruelty of evolution. Such an argument sounds cynical in my ears.

Then you have misunderstood me in a basic way. I neither wish to justify the behavior of Yasutani Roshi and Harada Roshi or the thought patterns that led to that behavior. Let me state things unequivocally: I consider it completely erroneous to derive a social ideology from a structural principle of evolution. That would hardly be acceptable, at least for a person with a mystical consciousness. Such a person—if he or she is a genuine mystic—must stand up for the very opposite: for peace. That would be the logical consequence of an experience of unity with all living things. If the person fails to come to that conclusion, either no genuine experience has taken place or it has faded over time, having become covered with conditioning from childhood.

In other words, someone who has had a mystical experience is not necessarily a better person as a result.

It depends on the depth of the experience and the question of what is better and what is worse. It's very difficult to set up global norms for all of humanity.

Is there any sense at all, from a mystical standpoint, in using categories like "better" or "worse"?

The quality of an action is not dependent on the good or bad will of the acting subject. It depends solely on whether the action arises from a mystical experience of unity or not. If it does, it is pervaded by an all-embracing love for all creatures, a love that is not wished or sought, but which appears by itself. When this love flourishes it becomes the single binding norm for behavior. It becomes the yardstick for everything we do. This doesn't mean that the person who loves in that way tries to please everybody. Love can also be severe. A mother takes the scissors away from her child when she senses danger—no matter how much the child cries and screams.

You're suggesting that mystical experience leads us beyond the sphere of morality. If that's true, it would seem that, from a mystical viewpoint, concepts such as "guilt" and "sin," so important in Christianity, are bereft of content.

From the mystical standpoint sin is in the final analysis nothing more than a lack of realization. Those who have realized their true essence and who have let go of their ego-fixation in entering the transpersonal sphere will behave ethically. They will realize that moral regulations and ethical commandments arise from love. Sin simply consists of refusing this love and self-transcendence while remaining stuck in our ego-structures. Sin is a state of separation, a state of self-exclusion of the ego from the stream of love. And when this self-exclusion gets out of hand, ruin lurks in the shadows. In this connection I'd like to direct our attention once again to science, which insists that closed systems incapable of opening themselves to their environment are doomed to perish. We can observe the same phenomenon in the field of social history. A society will inevitably fade from the stage of history if it is only concerned with itself and neglects communication with the outside. Greek mythology uses the story of Narcissus to illustrate this principle. It's the story of a beautiful youth so infatuated by his own beauty that it became his downfall.

The classical story of sin is no doubt the one in the Book of Genesis about the loss of paradise. Could we say it also deals with the "original sin" of refusing self-transcendence?

It tells the history up to that event. It shows us how we could get into a situation where we refuse self-transcendence. In that biblical account, the actual fall from grace is nothing more than the step into individuation, the withdrawal from a "prepersonal heaven." It deals with our awakening from a vague preconsciousness to an experience of the ego. It's about emerging from an instinctual state to one in which we recognize good and evil. That was a major step forward in evolution, although accompanied by considerable additional burdens that began to oppress us the moment we became aware of our individual selves. Those burdens include death, sickness, suffering, guilt, and isolation.

That's a rather unusual reading of the story of the Fall.

Perhaps, but there's the added advantage that the message of salvation is revealed in the story. Sin is not a matter of eating from the tree of knowledge of good and evil. Sin happened when the human beings, with their emerging awareness of a separate self, turned away from God, that is, from their true essence. "They were naked," it says in the Scriptures. This has nothing to do with having no clothes on. It means we were cast out into the isolation of our ego. The expulsion from paradise is the emergence into the personal state of consciousness. It is the emergence of the ego-consciousness out of a state of unity with God. Seen in this way, sin is not the individual trespasses of individual persons; it is the price humanity has to pay for individuation. We live in this sin as long as we remain unable to transcend ourselves in mystical experience. The spiritual path is thus the way into paradise—but not the paradise from which we were banned. To regress to that state would be tantamount to crawling back into the womb of evolution. But evolution should bring us forward. One day we will realize that God has always been walking with us in the Garden of Eden, that we were never really separated from him and just didn't realize it. Paradise is right in front of us. Christians call it the "New Jerusalem," which means the experience of unity with God.

In that sense, the "New Jerusalem" would be a world where only mystics dwell? There would be no need for norms and commandments.

Even then we will still have to erect traffic signs and traffic lights at intersections. We'll still need to decide on rules to get along with one another. But those rules will emerge from a deeper source of knowledge. In our earthly existence, we humans will be dependent on ethical norms and commandments, as well as justice and laws. They provide us with the necessary "rules of the game" to organize our interactions within society. That has little to do with religion.

But one can't help questioning the religious basis of norms and commandments if their legitimacy is questioned. Don't our moral ideas ultimately have a religious core?

If you trace the history of morality back to its origins, you eventually arrive at the founders of the religions. That leads me to conclude that the key statements regarding morality in all cultures and religions are nourished by mystical experiences. Their common source is the transpersonal sphere, which, by the way, also explains the high degree of agreement among religions in matters of morality. The norms and commandments of the founders were originally nothing more than instructions for a life in keeping with the reality of God that they had experienced. In the course of time, however, those instructions came free of their spiritual roots and took on a life of their own. Morality became its own aim. And when that happens, questions of its legitimacy necessarily arise.

In Buddhism there is the Eightfold Path, in Christianity the Ten Commandments and the Sermon on the Mount. Were these norms originally instructions for a spiritual life? Do we reach God in obeying those commandments?

It'd be safe to say that it's helpful for spiritual practice to lead an orderly life. It would be counterproductive if I were to place myself in opposition to the rules of society or my own health when practicing a spiritual path. I'd be distracting myself far too much from the essential matter. I would no longer be capable of devoting myself fully to the spiritual path. Likewise, there will be actions and behaviors that we avoid because we realize them to be obstructions to spiritual practice. These are the things we experience as "evil" or "bad" because they block the way to realization. The list of such obstructions extends from egocentricity to the various forms of addiction.

An altruistic set of ethics like those in Christianity, oriented toward one's fellow human beings, must certainly be welcome from the standpoint of mysticism because they encourage a way of behaving that is not ego-fixated. Can Christian morality offer us aid along the spiritual path?

Yes and no. A commandment like "Love your neighbor as yourself" certainly brings about a state in which our ego-fixation is reduced. But that positive effect can be negated if we obey the commandment simply for its own sake and not for the sake of others. When that happens, morality becomes a hindrance to spirituality, not as a result of the actions that it forbids but because of the rewards it promises. Ethics don't have their origin in commandments. They belong to the basic structure of evolution. They amount to a natural law deriving from love. In the final analysis, ethics are nothing more than agreement with the principle of self-transcendence and love. They are a result of an experience of God.

Christian morality involves not only commandments but also prohibitions. You, as a Christian monk, have taken vows of poverty and chastity. How do you bring this aspect into agreement with your conviction that it is the responsibility of the human being to be human? Can essential areas like sexuality simply be ignored?

Renunciation for the sake of a higher goal can be very meaningful. When I climb a mountain, I leave a lot of things, even important things, at home. In some situations I leave something behind to gain something more meaningful. Everyone is free to choose the type of life he or she considers best. That can mean marriage or life in a monastic community. Vows have a positive significance for life in such a community. Thus it's only natural to observe them.

And what about life outside the monastery?

Even for people who don't live in a monastery it can be meaningful to give up possessions and sexuality, if they are so disposed. For what is the purpose of the vows? The sole purpose is to eliminate anything that prevents us from arriving at an all-encompassing realization. Only in this does asceticism have meaning. When it becomes an aim in itself, it can cause a lot of damage. Unfortunately that has happened all too often in the past. In his sermons, Meister Eckhart railed against an exaggerated asceticism widespread in his day that included hair shirts and self-flagellation.

But do you believe, then, that physical austerities can be meaningful to a certain extent on the spiritual path?

Only if the body appears to be a hindrance on the spiritual path. And even then it is totally out of place to violently chastise the body. You have to discover where the problems lie with the body and deal with those problems, perhaps with therapy. Basically, however, the body is something in which God wants to be human. In Zen we know that mystical experience can occur in the bath, on the toilet, during sex, or when chopping wood. The divine reveals itself in everything, and always when we have been gifted with being able to let go.

Is that the reason why we encounter texts by women medieval mystics or in Bernhard of Clairvaux describing the mystical experience in erotic language?

People who have had a deep experience dissolve into an all-embracing love where there is neither "I love you" nor "I love God." By pervading everything, love levels off all "I-Thou" distinctions. In wishing to express that love in words, it often happens, especially in Christianity, that it is personalized as love of God or love of Jesus. The love then has an "other," and in that moment the mystical experience can assume an erotic character.

But isn't that in the nature of things? After all, a love relationship inevitably involves two separate entities.

Yes, but the actual essence of love is found in the fact that these two transcend their respective egos in a higher unity. It is not the duality of the lovers, not their dialogue that counts. The essential element is the act of love itself. Rumi (1207–1273) saw this very clearly and wrote in one of his poems: "Here I am with you, and you want to read letters. That's not the essence of true love." What he's saying is: I'm right here, and despite that fact, you're writing love letters to me. We could continue and say: I'm here, and despite that fact, you're reading to me out of your prayer book. The presence of the beloved is not even noticed. We're terrified of such a union. That's different with mystical love, where there is only unity. I ask myself why there is such a fear of union.

But the erotic language of the female mystics leads us to assume that it expresses the transcendence of duality in mystical union.

Interestingly enough, many people have a very nondramatic experience of unity, while others experience a burning, even erotic type of love. The fact that the same thing happened to the medieval women mystics certainly has to do with their use of the language of the minnesingers or medieval bards of courtly love, a type of poetry that was not sexual in the narrow sense. It was eroticism that was aware it would not find sexual fulfillment. This is a fascinating fact that can teach us moderns not a few things. In our corner of the world, there is no form of relationship between man and woman other than marriage that wouldn't be considered suspicious from the outset. Such mystical eroticism shows us that things don't necessarily have to be that way.

Clearly, quite a few things appear different from the mystical perspective compared to the perspective of our conventional worldview. Please allow me to become a bit more concrete at the end of our discussion as we turn our attention to some of the ethical questions that particularly concern and interest people of today. The first area is medical ethics, a very problematic field. What do you consider to be the most important characteristics of a meaningful medical ethics, from the point of view of the mystical understanding of the human being?

Mysticism's basic tenet is: There is neither being born nor dying. There is only continuation of the single reality, of the single divine life, which is structured and manifested repeatedly in millions of forms both known and unknown to us. It is this conviction that distinguishes the mystical worldview from our everyday understanding, which is incidentally also the understanding of most religions. Christianity announces the resurrection of the dead, but a look at our cemeteries is enough to realize that belief in life everlasting is not very widespread among Christians.

But in the Credo that we recite Sunday after Sunday we profess our faith in the resurrection.

Yes, but resurrection has a completely different meaning in this connection. In the dualistic worldview of Christianity, there is God and there are people. Here, resurrection means that God awakens us somewhere else in a distant future. This notion of resurrection implies persistence of the ego beyond death, a most unsatisfying idea. Mysticism, on the other hand, sees resurrection as the very opposite of such a persistence of the individual self over time. It is letting go of ego in becoming one with the primary reality, with God. We are manifestations of this primary reality, and because that remains beyond the death of the individual, we can justly believe in a resurrection. But it is not a resurrection of the individual ego, but a resurrection in a transpersonal unity with God.

What does that mean for a doctor facing the question of whether or not he should keep a terminally ill person alive by artificial means?

In such a situation I would always advise the doctor to let life takes its course. If a life wishes to come to an end, then we should allow it to do so. We shouldn't attempt to maintain life artificially by resorting to different devices. If more doctors would observe this simple truth, we could avoid a lot of problems in the intensive care units. Of course, it's the doctor who must decide in each case. If it's a case of a young person with his life before him, the doctor will do everything he can to keep him alive. But if it's an old person whose "time is near," then there's certainly no sense in that person struggling with death for two or three days longer.

But doctors who try to keep patients alive are only acting according to our view of the person. In Western society death is an evil to be avoided at all costs.

I certainly don't want to condemn our doctors. They're simply responding as society expects them to. But that says nothing about the quality of this view of the person. Other cultures believe that death is a beginning and not an end.

Should we allow euthanasia?

Yes and no. If fully conscious people with no hope of recovery wish to take their leave, we shouldn't attempt artificial means to lengthen their lives. I see no sense in forcing people to live against their will. But we shouldn't shorten life willfully. Experience has shown that remaining alive in such situations can often be very meaningful. People who are terminally ill are often ready for an inner transformation that they would otherwise have shrunk away from.

Science makes unimaginable efforts to outwit death. Incredible advances are expected in the field of genetic technology. The possibility increases of lengthening life by altering genetic material or saving the individual genetic substance for future generations by cloning. While some people dream of a future when we will live forever, others are concerned, seeing here an affront to the dignity of the person. How can we judge genetic technology from the standpoint of mysticism?

Genetic technology's triumphal march cannot be stopped. If genes can be manipulated, people will apply the necessary technology to do so. If people can be cloned, they will be cloned. Attempts will be made to breed human beings. Maybe we'll get our fingers burnt in the process, but that won't stop genetic researchers. Humanity has misused everything it has discovered, starting with the wheel right on up the atom. We're bound to try it with genes as well.

But wouldn't that amount to unauthorized intervention in evolution?

Given how we've been provided with a mind, we've become something like co-creators. There are no rules saying we have to let evolution run its course. On the contrary, I am convinced that we *can* interfere in evolution since we have the possibility of doing so. Nevertheless, a prerequisite is that our practical faculties of judgment are not dependent on the technical possibilities. I see a major discrepancy here at present between judgment and possibilities—and this is what worries me.

Does that mean, in your opinion, that there is no reason to mobilize politically and socially against genetic technology?

I'm working with the inner person, although I hope my work will also be relevant for the outer person. If we cannot bring people to develop a sense of responsibility based on their inner convictions, any law will remain relative and subject to violation. It would be important to devote our energies to ensuring that new forms of technology are used in a responsible manner. It's a question of conscience in this case. Conscience is the basic tendency in evolution to open ourselves to others. If this basic tendency is obscured, laws can only have a limited effect. I see my task as one of making this basic tendency of love come alive.

Are there other areas of political life where mystically inspired persons should engage themselves?

I've already spoken of engagement on behalf of peace. Ecology also appears to me to be such a field. The mystical experience of unity is not limited to kinship with other people, but with all of nature. People practicing a spiritual path develop a greater awareness of others and of their environment. This is often evident in a new relationship to animals and plants, a feeling of closeness to nature. Mysticism and kinship with all life are two sides of the same coin.

CHAPTER 7

"Demons" Can Be Helpers

Why Mysticism Serves
the Welfare of All

Many people come to you hoping for physical or psychological improvement in their lives. Does mysticism make us healthier?

Almost all the great mystics—including Teresa of Ávila, John of the Cross, Hildegard of Bingen—suffered from illness. That would seem to indicate that mysticism doesn't necessarily make you any healthier. It is nevertheless correct that spiritual experiences, like other psychological processes, have an effect on our physical and psychological condition. But illnesses originating from genetic defects cannot be prevented or cured by spiritual practices alone. We can, at best, influence the conditions under which those illnesses occur. For this reason there have been greater efforts in alternative medicine to develop new forms of therapy, especially in treating cancer. Meditation and imagination play a major role in such therapy forms. For example, patients are instructed to imagine that positive forces are attacking the illness and overcoming it. Evidently some success has been possible with such methods.

How do we explain that?

In one of our earlier discussions we spoke about "morphogenetic fields," that is, spiritual, a-causal fields that are responsible for the ordering and shaping of cosmic life in individual organisms. These fields are not only found in individual forms of life. They influence and organize all of reality. And they always occur when spiritual energy has gathered together in a new constellation. I wouldn't be surprised if this can occur by means of imagination and meditation.

Would that be an explanation for the miraculous cures reported in places of pilgrimage devoted to the Blessed Virgin?

Miraculous cures, or "remissions" as they are known in medical circles, cannot be refuted. It's been shown that individuals or groups can create healing and helping energies. They can open themselves to divine energy and become an instrument for it. The emptier and open a person is, the more he or she is suited as an instrument of healing. The healing energy then only needs to be allowed to flow to take effect. Anyone who radiates good will or love creates a helping, healing, and ordering field. That is a natural law on a higher level. It does not require praying to God in another world. I traveled often with an African bishop who was the son of a tribal medicine man and who had "inherited" the gift of healing from his father. More than once, I witnessed how disturbed persons who believed themselves to be possessed by spirits were healed by him. However, I cannot judge how long such spontaneous cures had an effect. That's often the problem. In many cases only the symptoms are eliminated. The actual cause of the illness remains, so that the symptoms can reoccur.

Do I understand you correctly that actually everyone should be capable of such "miraculous cures"?

The progression of evolution has not yet come so far as for everyone to have the necessary transparency for such healing energies. But they are nevertheless there for us all. Many people, like my friend in Africa, seem to have a natural disposition for such powers; others develop by means of a long process of spiritual practice the inner readiness by which such energies can take effect. There's much untapped potential in us that we've yet to discover. We don't need these abilities for our immediate survival. They are waiting to be released and activated at a later stage in the development of consciousness.

What specific potential do you have in mind?

There are healers capable of discerning what physical ailments a person is suffering from by examining distortions in that person's aura. Their diagnoses have been checked with standard medical testing devices with amazing results. I'm certain we have the potential for telepathy, telekinesis, and many other abilities of which we have no idea. Evolution progresses in us and releases new abilities and possibilities.

Can sick persons be healed by prayers?

If I pray in a spirit of goodwill and love for other people, a healing and helping energy field can develop that has an effect beyond space and time. You can activate such an energy field by praying to a Madonna figure, lighting a candle, or going on a pilgrimage.

I notice no mention of God in this description of prayer.

Prayers don't have their effect because God, Mary, or a guardian angel in heaven hears my prayers and responds with aid. With the help of their images, however, an energy field is created that has a soothing and healing effect. This is not only true in the Christian tradition; it's equally true for Buddhists or shamans. I lived in Japan for six years next to a place of pilgrimage dedicated to the Bodhisattva Kannon. Kannon is an archetype of compassion to which people pray, light candles or incense, or leave offerings in times of need. I would be hard put to find any difference between that temple and a place of pilgrimage for Marian devotion.

We've already spoken about how, from the mystical standpoint, our view of the world and humanity is transformed. Does that also hold for our understanding of concepts to "sickness" and "health"?

More important than "sickness" or "health" from the viewpoint of mysticism is the concept expressed in the German word *Heil.* Related to the English words *whole* and *hail* in the sense of good health, also in its psychological and spiritual aspects, even a so-called "sick" person can be "whole" (in the sense we're using the word here) while a so-called "healthy" person can be totally lacking in that quality.

But what does it mean "to be whole" in this sense of the word?

It means understanding the significance of your life and being able to interpret it accordingly. Your own life can still be meaningful even when the external circumstances are negative. This is why the concept of "*Heil*"—"whole," "hail"—includes a religious element. It grows out of the religious sphere, where alone the true dimension of meaning in our life is revealed. The spiritual path does not necessarily lead us through what we usually refer to as happiness. The way of healing and salvation can also lead through deprivation, sickness, and problems of all sorts, even death and the underworld.

Is happiness also a part of being "whole"?

If you are really "whole," you are surely happy—but not everyone who calls himself happy is necessarily "whole." What we usually refer to as happiness has a strong personal element. It is the ego that considers itself to be happy. Happiness for the ego means the absence of anything unpleasant and painful—it's the feeling that comes when reality agrees with our will. But that doesn't necessarily suffice for people to be "whole." I've met happy persons in wheelchairs and unhappy persons who could satisfy their every wish.

In viewing things from this holistic perspective, how would we define sickness, the complementary concept to "health" in this broader sense we are speaking about?

Actual sickness lies much deeper than the symptoms. We become sick when our basic physical needs are not satisfied. But we also become ill when we do not satisfy our basic spiritual needs. The tragic thing is that many people don't even sense their basic spiritual needs and therefore don't recognize the cause of their suffering. Viktor Frankl (1905–1997) thus speaks of a "noogenic neurosis," a neurosis that has its roots in the spirit. Abraham Maslow calls it a "metapathology."

What consequences will this new understanding have in the field of medicine? Should doctors be more disposed to choose a more holistic approach and place healing in a wider sense in the center rather than simple physical health?

Doctors should first learn from Socrates. In one of the Platonic dialogues, Socrates recounts how a young man named Charmides visited him and complained that his head was so heavy when he got up in the morning. And what does Socrates recommend to the young man?

> Our king, who is a god, says that as you ought not to attempt to cure eyes without head, or head without body, so you should not treat body without soul; and this was the reason why most maladies evaded the physicians of Greece—that they neglected the whole, on which they ought to spend their pains, for if this were out of order it was impossible for the part to be in order. For all that was good and evil, he said, in the body and in man altogether was sprung from the soul, and flowed along from thence as it did.[1]

Socrates believed that we shouldn't heal the symptoms of a sickness, but the entire person.

The idea, after all, of a "holistic approach" to medicine is no longer a foreign phrase for most doctors.

The insight that a sick person is more than a car requiring repairs so that it can run again after replacing the right parts is slowly gaining ground in the field of medicine. Sickness is understood more and more as symptoms in a larger context that includes the psychological and spiritual dimensions. This is indicative of the insight that religiosity and faith can have a major influence on the healing process. Researchers in the United States are evidently having success in showing empirically the connection between one's religious attitude and the chances for cure.

Nevertheless, there is considerable opposition in orthodox medicine against all forms of alternative therapy. The insights you mention do not seem to have found a real place in our medical schools.

Among the representatives of orthodox medicine, you find a disturbing number of "hardliners" who ridicule all forms of alternative medicine. I myself don't trust everything going on in the field of alternative medicine, but I don't categorically deny everything as a result. I believe that homeopathy, for example, is on the right track when it attempts to heal illness not with nonmaterial information instead of physical materials. In that sense it agrees much more with a mystical view of the person than orthodox medicine.

What other forms of therapy seem meaningful to you from the standpoint of mysticism?

All those approaches that understand the person as a totality, and which look for the psychological and spiritual causes of an illness behind the physical symptoms.

Is that true also for psychotherapy? Is psychotherapy a way of healing particularly close to mysticism?

Classical psychology has an ambivalent relationship to mysticism. It can prepare the way for mystical experience, but it can also stand in its way. Many attempts at therapy aim solely to stabilize the ego. The goal is to free the ego from blockages and complexes so it can function in its social environment. But that's obviously not enough for a cure in the true sense. C. G. Jung already realized that our actual problems lie much deeper, that they result from our often futile attempts to find meaning in our lives. In this connection he says:

> Among all my patients in the second half of life—that is to say, over age thirty-five—there has not been one whose problem in the last resort was not that of finding a religious outlook on life. It is safe to say that every one of them fell ill because he had lost what the living religions of every age have given to their followers, and none of them has really been healed who did not regain his religious outlook. This of course has nothing to do with a particular creed or membership of a church.[2]

How do you explain these findings?

Up to middle age, people are outwardly oriented and project their expectations for salvation in that direction: Finding a marriage partner, sex, power, money, career, and the like, cover over a search for meaning and a striving for fulfillment. This inner striving can then break out in midlife in a most elementary way. The task of psychotherapy then moves from the traditional goal of stabilizing the ego toward the spiritual problem of finding meaning in our lives.

Although that can't be separated from conventional psychology.

As is true for medicine, considerable changes have occurred in the past thirty years in the field of psychology. Transpersonal psychology has emerged as a new branch that attempts to heal by going beyond the ego-consciousness to release healing powers in the domain of the transpersonal consciousness. The American psychotherapist A. H. Almaas (born 1944), for example, says that a cure is only possible when the patient has experienced himself in his transpersonal identity, when he opens up a new dimension of meaning, on the horizon of which he can interpret and understand his own biography.

What differentiates transpersonal psychology from conventional psychology?

Transpersonal psychology divides the spectrum of consciousness into various regions: the prepersonal, personal, and transpersonal areas of consciousness. This final area of consciousness is further divided by Ken Wilber into the minute, causal, and cosmic consciousness. Cosmic consciousness is the level of mysticism. Conventional psychology, on the other hand, only recognizes the personal consciousness. Entry into the transpersonal sphere of consciousness cannot be achieved by scientifically provable means. Science thus refutes this transcendent region and calls it superstition. For the most part, general scientific opinion reflects the reaction of Sigmund Freud to a letter his friend Romain Rolland sent him from India. In his letter, Rolland describes a mystical experience, but Freud, in attempting to introspect himself, fails to find anything in any way similar to what his friend describes.

How are these various spheres of consciousness in transpersonal psychology related to one another?

Just as a rainbow spreads the spectrum of a single light beam out like a fan, the single divine consciousness develops in the plurality of the forms of consciousness. This development occurs in evolution. In the cosmic framework it progresses from preconsciousness through the personal consciousness to the cosmic consciousness. According to Jean Gebser, whom I cited above, our consciousness has evolved from preconsciousness into magical consciousness, and from magical consciousness into mythical consciousness, and finally mental consciousness. We stand today on the threshold of a further level of consciousness. Our personal welfare and the continuation of our species will depend largely on whether we can successfully take that next step.

What methods does transpersonal psychology use to cure people of psychological ailments?

There is a wide range of therapy forms that consider the transpersonal sphere to be a source of healing. The so-called systemic therapy of Bert Hellinger (born 1925) has proven to be a helpful preparation for further therapy. It can help uncover complex entanglements and areas of dependency—especially in families—and to defuse problems through a careful reprocessing of things. Many people don't even live their own lives, but function unconsciously as deputies for some relative or ancestor. A major strength of systemic therapy is its ability to uncover these relationships and thus create room for a more individual, responsible life. Other forms of therapy create states of consciousness in which repressed or submerged complexes and fears come up to the surface where they can be treated. In this respect, Stanislav Grof (born 1931), a man who has studied the transpersonal sphere for many years and developed various therapeutic approaches, has done us a great service. Among his techniques is "holotropic breathing" in which the ego-consciousness is opened by means of an enrichment of the organism with oxygen. That can happen in two directions: either "forward" into the transpersonal sphere or "backward" into a prepersonal state of consciousness where we experience again our own birth or long-forgotten childhood traumas. In the ensuing therapeutic interview, those experiences can be examined and processed. In both cases it is important that the therapist also understands himself as a spiritual companion, a fact that Grof has very clearly seen and supported. One thing common to these forms of therapy, at any rate, is their ability to let us see through various forms of conditioning, thus freeing us from entanglements. They don't do this in a purely cognitive manner, as in conventional client-centered therapy, but place the persons back in the situations where their neuroses or psychic wounds had their origin. By experiencing and suffering through those situations once again, those forms of conditioning can lose their power over us.

What is the relationship between the forms of therapy you just described and mystical spirituality?

These therapies constitute a meaningful supplement. In many cases, inner blockages, such as those resulting from childhood traumas must be eliminated prior to taking our first steps on the spiritual path. Time and again in my contemplation courses, participants have the frustrating experience of the same childhood traumas arising in their consciousness with incredible tenacity over a period of eight days. That's hardly surprising, for "when the stage is free, the devils start to dance." In such cases I often recommend students to undergo psychotherapy to become aware of where they still remain stuck. Mystical spirituality does not eliminate the need for psychology. Indeed, the mystical path often calls on the aid of psychology to aid people in creating a coherent ego-structure that can act as the basis for further progress on the spiritual path. In mysticism this is known as "the way of purification."

In that sense, conventional psychotherapy would be a kind of preparatory course for the spiritual path.

It can assume that role, although we shouldn't reduce psychotherapy to that function alone. Conventional psychotherapy has its fullest justification and greatest strength in dealing with personality disorders such as those originating in family entanglements, psychic wounds, or life crises. Psychotherapy can be successful and meaningful in those areas. It's a different story, however, when the psychological problems are more deeply rooted, such as those resulting from a spiritual crisis. In such cases, traditional psychotherapy quickly reaches its limits, since true healing here can only come from the transpersonal sphere, an area closed to conventional psychology. Although, on the one hand, the transpersonal experience understands all ego-structures to be relative, it leads, on the other hand, to self-worth, which is helpful for our ego-structure. Along the spiritual path we experience how life "breaks through," so to speak. It's like a cherry tree blooming. Where only bare branches were yesterday, we now see thousands of shining white blossoms. You can't force something like that. It comes from within. The experience of total reality is also a breaking open of life from within. An old Chinese saying expresses this aptly: "I asked the almond tree to tell me about God and it began to bloom." People should be able to say that about themselves. It's a matter of starting to be all we are. It concerns nothing more and nothing less than our full humanity. We've become human beings so we can grow and ripen to a more all-embracing existence. That is the actual reason we are here. The real sin or transgression is simply neglecting our "homework" in life. Perhaps that's what the Bible is talking about when it speaks of a "sin against the Holy Spirit."

If genuine spiritual healing can only come from the transpersonal sphere, close cooperation between classical psychology and transpersonal psychology would appear meaningful. What efforts are being made in that respect?

Spiritual Emergency Network is the name of a movement that started in the United States and which has since spread to Europe. Therapists have joined forces to consciously integrate the spiritual dimension in their work. I can also say that I hardly know a clinic today treating psychosomatic disorders that doesn't also offer meditation. The powers of the transpersonal sphere are used for healing. But they can also cause the opposite of healing if not aware of the dangers involved. People can also enter psychotic states where they are no longer in control. We characterize psychosis as "disease." To me, however, it appears, at least to some extent, to be something like "an experiment of evolution" in which we attempt to feel out new levels of consciousness, but which we let fall because they cannot— or not yet—be lived out.

Are you saying that psychotics are simply people living "at the wrong time"?

Perhaps it would be better to say, "In the wrong world." In our present world, psychotics will hardly be able to prevail in evolution. That's why Joseph Campbell is right when he says that initially there is no difference between the psychotic and the mystic. Both of them have entered the sea of consciousness. The only difference is that a mystic can swim and a psychotic can't. In contrast to the psychotic, the mystic has not lost the "lifesaver" of his ego-structure that he can always reach for and that he absolutely requires in organizing and giving a structure to all the psychic energies that force their way upon him.

What we now refer to as "psychic energies" were known in former times as "demons." You address the idea of demons in your books, attempting to give that idea a new meaning. What are demons all about?

Demons, shadows, devils, monsters—we have many different names for this psychological complexity that we find in all persons, even in Jesus. Recall the story of the temptation of Christ. It is no coincidence that the story takes place in the desert. The desert is the epitome of spiritual seclusion. Everyone who travels the path of contemplation goes "into the desert," so to speak, to be confronted with their shadow. Evagrius of Pontus, a fourth-century monk who left behind a considerable body of writings about the spirituality of monks living in the desert, describes demons that torment the practitioner when he enters solitude. He says we have to expect that the demon who leaves us on the left side during contemplation will return on the right side. In other words, psychological torments and difficulties can appear in our consciousness along the spiritual path, where they can be quite persistent.

Where do these "demons" come from?

"Demons" or "shadows" are that side of our consciousness that is turned away from us. We're dealing here with the abovementioned traumas from childhood or marriage, as well as fear and depression of various origins. These psychological states are often suppressed from our consciousness; they're split off from our ego. "Split off" is the literal translation of the Greek word *daimon*. There is reason to believe that humans originally knew quite well what we were dealing with when one spoke of "demons": We were dealing with what we now refer to as "neurotic portions" in psychology. When these repressed parts come into our consciousness in concentrated form, they can develop such power that it is quite natural to personify them as demons. Quite frightening images—grotesque faces, animals, and monsters—can rise up from the depths of the psyche. It's a "bestiary" we are familiar with from the many paintings depicting the temptation of Saint Anthony (251–355) in the desert. It always concerns visions of things we cannot accept in ourselves, things we condemn in ourselves. This also explains the extraordinary tenacity of these "demons." They're a part of us we can't get rid of, and we will be less and less able to do so, the more we fight them.

But such "demonizing" doesn't only take the form of visionary projections on grotesque faces or fabulous creatures. It seems to me that they're much more often turned outward. In other words, we tend to condemn and "demonize" real persons more than imaginary "demons."

That's very true. First of all, we tend to project the shadow side of our consciousness toward the outside: toward the opposite sex, other races, other cultures, other religions, Jews, heathens, neo-Nazis, foreigners. In that way we "demonize" in others what we ought actually to recognize as a part of ourselves. Unfortunately such condemnation can also occur in the religious sphere. The difference between matter and spirit, body and consciousness, humankind and God, becomes an unbridgeable chasm. The body, sexuality, joy in nature and life are demonized and labeled "devilish." Here we have the start of religious fanaticism. This always happens when love is missing in a religion.

Faith without love—faith that cannot see and accept its own shadow—becomes fanaticism. C. G. Jung says that this projection toward the outside transforms one's environment into one's own unknown face. Then the others are the bad ones. Our first task, then, is to take back these projections and recognize the "bad" and "negative" elements in us in order to integrate them in our consciousness. In other words, we have to achieve the nearly impossible: seeing from where we are what's on the other side of the corner, as it were, and recognizing in ourselves the evil that we usually see in others outside of us.

Viewing things in that way, we're evidently dealing here with a process of healing for the soul if it no longer projects the "shadow" outwardly but produces visions of demons that also remind the consciousness internally of its suppressed aspects. Anything objectified in that way can be better integrated in actual life.

Precisely so. "Demons" should not be suppressed. The more we fight against them, the more power they have over us. Instead, we should accept them as a part of us and allow them to be present in our consciousness. That doesn't mean we have to live out these shadow sides of our personality. It's sufficient to admit them and accept them in order to then deal with them without being ruled by them. The *Tibetan Book of the Dead*, for example, deals with no other theme. It tells us how it is possible for a dying person to reach reconciliation between the fearful and friendly demons that delay the way of dying. Our task is to pass by both with composure, since remaining under their influence, in the Tibetan view, causes rebirth.

And is it on the spiritual path that we arrive at this composure?

That's how it should be. In any case, the path inevitably brings us to a point where we have to open ourselves to the shadow sides of the psyche. I've never met anyone in my contemplation courses who was not confronted during sitting meditation with all the things he or she had suppressed up to then. The first step occurs when we recognize the shadows. Then they can be integrated in our understanding of ourselves so they can eventually help us.

What does that mean in concrete terms for our spiritual practice?

It means that I encourage participants in my courses to take an offensive stance toward anything that comes up during their sitting meditation and not attempt to suppress it. "Look at it, accept it, let it happen! Don't judge it!" Sometimes I even say: "Talk with the images that come up. Ask them what they have to say to you! Make friends with your fear and your anger! They belong to you! They're life energy. You don't cut your toe off when it hurts you. Accept your sadness, but don't get carried away by it. Don't make a big thing of it. It's part of you. Look at it and then return to your practice." Sadness can be a good starting point for practice. The same is true about fear: "You don't know where it comes from and where it's been. But it's there. So say 'yes' to it. Say, 'yes, I'm afraid.'" Give it a place in your practice and allow it to disappear in that practice. We practice pure awareness, pure attention, without judging, without allowing ourselves to be carried away by our emotions. Emotions and fears have to be lived out. No commentary, no allowing yourself to get carried away with them, no struggling with them, no suppression. Emotions are like clouds floating by in the clear blue sky. They might darken the sky for a while, but eventually they disappear.

Then the decisive matter, in your opinion, is not identifying with our fears, emotions, psychic wounds, and the like?

Nonidentification with our feelings liberates us from our ego-fixation and opens our eyes to our true essence. It has nothing to do with suppression. I like to compare our emotions, moods, thoughts, and events to a storm on the ocean. What does the Atlantic Ocean care if a storm is raging in the Bay of Biscay? It's a matter of riding out the storm until it's over. The less we identify with the storm, the less power it has over us. But that doesn't mean we aren't able to feel our emotions anymore. It just means there is a still center under the surging storms of our psyche, a center that remains untouched by all that. We're no longer dominated by our emotions. We don't get carried away by them. Instead, they're transformed, and peace reigns in their place. Nevertheless, there is the danger then of a new identification with that state of peace. It's important then to let go of even that in a further step.

How can our emotions be transformed?

The transformation takes place when we create an inner distance to our emotions. If we're furious, we should be furious, but completely awake in our rage. Our anger should not suffocate our consciousness. If we're aware of our anger, it will slowly dissipate. It's stupid to run after your anger and try to live it out. The same is true for hatred or desire. You have to look them in the face and remain awake. Then you become free and realize that all these emotions are simply processes that pass like clouds through the psyche. In Zen, if a monk has a pleasant feeling, he knows "I'm having a pleasant feeling." If he has a painful feeling, he knows "I'm having a painful feeling." If he has a pleasant, worldly sensation, he knows "I'm having a pleasant, worldly sensation." If he has a pleasant, otherworldly sensation, he knows "I'm having a pleasant, otherworldly sensation." He stays with his practice and practices contemplation of his feelings, both inner and outer feelings. He remains in the original conditions of the feelings. His consciousness thus develops to a degree that is right for his feelings. He doesn't attach himself to anything in the world. That doesn't mean I can't show my emotions—others can and should feel my momentary displeasure—but it makes a big difference if I am simply reacting or I am acting as master of the situation.

Notes

1. Plato, *Charmides*, 156e.
2. *Collected Works of C.G. Jung, Volume 11: Psychology and Religion: West and East*, C.G. Jung, edited and translated by Gerhard Adler and R.F.C. Hull (Princeton, 1970), 509.

CHAPTER 8

Practice in the Art of Dying

Why Spiritual Teachers
Are Also Pastors

In this, our final discussion, I'd like to return once again to the question
of the degree to which mystical spirituality can help the person. We've
already attempted to clarify its relationship to psychology and medi-
cine. It became clear in that discussion that the spiritual path can
release healing energy. But I'm still not sure what role the spiritual teach-
er plays in that process. Could we also refer to such a teacher as a "pas-
toral counselor"?

They are not *just* counselors in that sense, but certainly *also* counselors. I've already described how people are often "catapulted" into
a mystical experience without any preparation for it, so that many
remain totally confused and disoriented. Their familiar worldview
has been destroyed and they now feel a great vacuum, causing them
to seek aid and support. They look for such help from psychothera-
pists and healers, but hardly ever from the Church. The German journal
Transpersonale Psychologie has released the findings of a study showing clearly what little competence is attributed to the clergy in such
matters.[1]

Is this mistrust a specifically Christian phenomenon? How do people in other religions handle such unexpected spiritual experiences?

In most other religions people who have been moved in the spiritual dimension seek out spiritual teachers for guidance. This leads to a student-teacher relationship that corresponds in many respects to the relationship between therapist and patient. In the Christian tradition there is the institution of the confessor or spiritual director who guides and supports the other person. This naturally requires a relationship characterized by mutual trust.

Confessors and spiritual directors have gone out of fashion by and large. What's the reason for this development?

That's not true. In the Catholic Church there are retreat masters who most certainly do accompany people on their spiritual journey. The question is just how capable they are of guiding persons who have had a mystical experience. John of the Cross, for example, complained bitterly about the inability of the spiritual directors of his times. He accuses them of being incapable of leading people into the mystical sphere when the time is ripe. Instead they attempted to steer those under their tutelage toward forms of prayer that were more a hindrance than a help. In his opinion, they left people in a lurch precisely at the point when difficulties and problems, the dryness and emptiness of the spiritual path, began. John of the Cross compared this situation with the exodus of the Israelites out of Egypt. God has done everything he could to lead his people out into the desert, and then come false teachers who want to make the fleshpots of slavery attractive to them again. Incidentally, the medieval German mystic Johannes Tauler arrived at a very similar appraisal of pastoral guides. Speaking about these spiritual directors, he says that these people—with their special pious practices, which they use to bring those people (meaning those on a spiritual path) to their side—create more hindrances to spiritual progress than any heathen ever did. Persons who judge with strong words and angry gestures should be careful when they speak about the inner person, he says. Pastoral counselors of our times should ask themselves if this criticism of Johannes Tauler isn't as timely today as it was five hundred years ago. It's extremely difficult to find people in the churches capable of guiding those searching for such guidance toward the mystical level. That's the reason I asked my community to allow me to practice with a Zen master in Japan. In Zen there is a living tradition of the "transmission of light," a transmission of the actual religious experience from teacher to disciple.

Such guidance of students by a spiritual master is obviously lacking in our Christian tradition. How does a spiritual master differ from a traditional theologian?

I don't like to use the terms student and master. I consider myself more like a companion along the way, like a mountain guide. If someone wants to climb a difficult mountain, he looks for someone who has already climbed it and who knows the way. A spiritual companion will thus make every effort to guide the student into a sphere where God can be experienced in an all-encompassing way, in a way that goes beyond a purely mental-rational meting out of knowledge as found in traditional theology. The companion on the way will initiate students in the practices of the spiritual way which we've spoken of already and will come to the aid of students as a counselor and partner in dialogue at difficult points along the way. The actual task of a spiritual guide, therefore, is to prepare people for the effects of grace and to help eliminate hindrances along the path so that they can experience the divine and experience spiritual development from the depths of their being.

Is it important for the spiritual guide to be an authority figure?

How the relationship between student and teacher develops depends on the persons in question. Important, however, is a clear understanding by both parties that this concerns a purely spiritual relationship. In such a relationship it is solely a matter of allowing the student to have a mystical experience, and indeed in a way that the teacher leads the student to his or her own inner source. John of the Cross said something definitive on this subject. There is the passage in his writings where he stresses that directors are not the chief agent, guide, and mover of souls in this matter, but the principal guide is the Holy Spirit.

What should people in search of a spiritual teacher have as guidelines?

There is no catalog of criteria you can give to someone in search of a teacher. Those wishing to embark on a spiritual path should visit different teachers and give careful consideration to the question of whose care they put themselves in. I advise people who come to me for guidance to first visit other teachers and attend other courses before deciding in favor of a particular teacher. No serious teacher demands that anyone become his or her student. If so, it would be a good reason for not becoming a student of that teacher!

Do you sometimes turn away someone who wishes to become your student?

Yes, indeed. If I have the impression after an initial meeting that an individual is still closely attached to a traditional understanding of religion, I will bring it to that person's attention that, in practicing the path that students learn under my guidance, many things that seemed most natural up to then will be seen in a new light. If someone shrinks back from such an encounter, I will refer that person to a teacher whom I consider better suited as a teacher. You also have to be very cautious about psychologically unstable persons. In such cases, I either advise them not to take up the practice or to undergo therapy as an adjunct to practice.

Do you also accept children and teenagers as students? Or do your people have to be a certain age before they can meaningfully embark on a spiritual path?

It's perfectly possible to undertake spiritual practice with teenagers. In Haus St. Benedikt we have a group called Education and Spirituality that is very interested in the question of how we can practice contemplation and meditation in the schools with children and teenagers.

It's important for that purpose to allow young people to find a form of spirituality in keeping with their mental set and feelings. Some schoolteachers have been able to create a quiet room in their schools where young people can retreat from time to time. The popularity of such rooms shows that they answer a real need among young people. Evidently the sensory overkill in the media creates a situation where peace and quiet are suddenly in demand. Aside from that, spiritual practice with young people is not that much different than that with adults. For young people, too, the main elements are concentration of mind and quieting the spirit, although young people evidently have an especially easy access to such concentration through the body.

What's a possible framework for meditation or contemplation courses in the schools?

Mainly through the religion classes or religious services in the schools. There should be the possibility for spiritual practice in religion class in addition to a purely cognitive imparting of knowledge. Religious education concerns the entire person, including his or her spiritual potential, an area that has been much neglected up to now. I consider this ignorance about spirituality to be the greatest failing of our educational system. We train young people's minds and reasoning powers for twelve to sixteen years, but lack a curriculum to develop areas in young people that can lead them to a much more all-encompassing experience than is possible with the intellect.

It appears that young people can really derive something from spiritual practices. What about older people? Is it possible even at eighty years of age to embark on a spiritual path?

You can start spiritual practices like those we've been discussing at any age. The only condition is the strong desire to devote yourself to the practice. Because such a desire often arises at critical junctures in life, it happens quite often that people come to me at the end of their careers who are now searching once again for a meaning in their lives. Often women in their forties want to embark on a spiritual path as the children are no longer living at home.

What do you say to older persons who maintain they are too old to start something like spiritual practice?

No one is too old for spiritual practice. If someone wants to sit on a chair to meditate, he or she is free to do so. There is no upper age limit on the spiritual path. We have people over eighty in our courses.

Are there differences in the way you instruct people, depending on their age?

The teaching should always be geared toward the individual personality. Age plays no role in that respect. Older people might even have an advantage, since they're not as restless as younger people. They can come to stillness more easily.

Do you also give people advice about what spiritual path it would be advisable to take up, such as Zen or Christian contemplation?

If I see that the individual has a positive and meaningful relationship to Christian faith, I will advise that person to choose the way of contemplation. If the individual has no religious background or interest in religion, I will recommend the Zen way or another Eastern path.

When you have accepted someone as a student, what does instruction consist of in concrete terms? How often do you meet with students?

I ask them to participate at least twice a year in a longer course. In addition, I advise them to maintain contact with me by visiting me from time to time. And of course it's very important that they take time each day for contemplative prayer or practice. Aside from that, my students can contact me at any time. I often offer personal interviews in the morning between 7:00 and 8:00 A.M.

How much importance do you give to acquiring theoretical knowledge on the spiritual path? Is it important to read books or listen to lectures?

The theoretical aspect of practice is secondary. In the beginning it's better not to read much. We have to learn the practice from the inside, not from the outside. That requires actual practice. It's only when you've had some experience in the practice that it becomes advisable to turn to books that can answer your growing need for a deepening of your practice.

Have you ever been in a situation of having to stop or temporarily discontinue a teaching relationship with a student?

That can happen, for example, when I see that someone is having psychological difficulties in practice or when it's not been possible to establish a necessary relationship of trust.

How can you prevent something like that from happening?

A spiritual relationship should always concentrate on the essential matter: the spiritual path itself and the difficulties that students encounter on the way. If that is not the case, or if it is no longer the case, it is better to part ways.

Does that mean you don't attempt to advise people about their concrete life situations?

Yes, I do. For example, problems often occur that are connected with difficulties in the family or one's marriage relationship. These problems rise to the surface of consciousness during contemplation. Women, for example, often come to realize that, up to then, they have only lived their lives in service to others. They then find the courage for a new start in life. That can sometimes lead to marital conflicts.

What help can you give to persons in such a situation?

I first explain in no uncertain terms that I am not a marriage counselor or family therapist and that I do not wish to attempt anything that should rightly be in the hands of a therapist. But in many cases it is actually spiritual problems that separate people. Let me give you an example. Not too long ago a couple came to me who were about to celebrate their twenty-fifth anniversary. Each of them was, in his or her own way, following a spiritual path, but they had a problem which therapy had not helped to solve. They didn't know whether they should use their twenty-fifth anniversary as an occasion for going their separate ways or for attempting a new start.

After I talked with them and discussed the matter of their spiritual practice, they decided in favor of a new start. We then celebrated a ritual that gave a special meaning to this new start. Of course, the opposite can also happen. A marriage or relationship can run into difficulties because one of the persons is intensively involved in a spiritual practice. If the two people decide to separate, it is important to have a ritual that helps them achieve the separation in good will and without mutual blame. That is far better for all those concerned than legal proceedings in a divorce court.

What effect do the rituals you've just mentioned have?

Rituals are helpful in two ways. First, they help to anchor more securely in a person a decision made on the rational level. With a ritual, that step can be experienced with the senses and with the body. This gives the decision a concreteness that makes it easier to come to terms with the new situation. It's often important to reconcile yourself with your wounds. This has nothing to do with suppression. The wounds can be felt, but they're no longer a cause of continual friction robbing us of any joy in life. Sometimes I carry out a ritual in which I urge persons plagued by hatred and pain to write down everything that pains them. When that's done, their notes are committed to the fire in a ritual burning ceremony. This is a more meaningful expression of how self-reproach and mutual blame now have an end.

And what is the second use of such rituals?

They make it possible to externalize inner feelings. The persons in question can then achieve a healing distance from their own emotions. They stop identifying with those feelings. Now they can allow those feelings to be, without having to be under their yoke. Now they can have feelings, the feelings don't have them. Incidentally, that's also true about positive feelings. Rituals can be helpful in giving expression to this totally different aspect of reality that we've experienced. That occurs in the form of religious ceremonies. They emphasize how all of life should actually be pervaded with an experience of the divine. They also remind us that religion is to be lived in everyday life. Life is a celebration. Mysticism means: I celebrate my life as a form of expressing the divine. God wishes to become human in us.

This can only happen with an awareness of our own mortality, which is precisely what most people shy away form. Death is seen as evil itself, as something we're so afraid of that it has to be suppressed continually. Can mystical spirituality make a contribution to reducing our fear of death?

A true mystical experience leads to the insight that there is actually no death. That which dies is simply the form in which the essential expresses itself. Being born and dying are nothing more than the beginning and end of a particular manifestation of the primary reality. The reality itself is not touched in the least. Being born and dying occur in every moment of evolution. God is that coming-and-going. This human form of ours will also fall away and a new form will come into existence. It is not important whether it has an identity with the old forms. It is always only the primary reality that is incarnated, the reality we refer to as God. That knows no change, no time, no space. Time and space exist only in the forms that come and go. Let me relate a short anecdote in this connection that has been rewritten for modern times.

I'm all ears.

An old woman was ironing clothes. The angel of death appeared to her and said, "It is time. Come with me!" The woman answered, "OK, but first I have to finish ironing the clothes. Who's going to do it in my place? And I have to cook dinner. My daughter is working in the office. She has to have something to eat when she comes home. Don't you understand?" The angel went away. A while later he came again. He met the woman just as she was leaving the house. "Come!" he said. "It is time!" The woman answered, "But I have to go to the nursing home first. A dozen people are waiting there for me who've been forgotten by their families. I can't leave them in a lurch!" The angel went away again. A while later he returned and said, "It is time! Come with me!" The woman answered, "OK, OK, I know, but who's going to bring my grandchild to kindergarten when I'm not here?" The angel sighed and said, "OK, I'll wait until your grandson can go alone to kindergarten." A few years later the woman was sitting one evening in front of her house, feeling tired and thinking, "The angel of death could actually come for me now. After that grind, bliss must be wonderful." The angel came and the woman asked, "Are you going to bring me to eternal bliss?" Now it was the angel's turn to ask: "And where do you think you've been all the time?"

What does this story have to tell us?

It tells us that the true reality is always here in this moment. There is only this timeless dance that life carries out in evolution. The meaning of the dance is not found in its coming to an end. It's found in the dance itself. The meaning of the dance is found in living the life of God moment by moment. But no one can realize that by reason alone. We can only experience it directly in mystical experience. And when that happens, our fear of death disappears. For, why should we be afraid of death when we know our true essence can neither be born nor die? Why should we be afraid that the ship will sink when God is the ocean into which it sinks?

There is a wonderful saying attributed to Socrates, which says that philosophy is nothing more than practice in dying. Can we say the same thing about mysticism?

Yes, although dying for the mystic—letting go of the ego—is much more difficult than physical dying. Dying for the mystic is dying that does not worry about how or whether anything happens in another world. It is dying into something much larger, where the question about the further existence of the personality no longer exists. It is a dying that Jesus set the example for when he said, "Father, into your hands I commend my spirit." There is no longing for heaven or hoping to be sheltered in God. There is only this letting go of the inessential.

What is the inessential?

The inessential is the ego, the ego that is seen in its relativity in an experience of the transpersonal reality. For there we enter a state of consciousness where there is no longer an ego, although probably aware and present. From this perspective the ego appears as what it actually is: an organization and function center for our earthly existence. Thus the ego's fear of death is justified. It will disappear, although it has been created to prevent such a disappearance of life. It has been created for the dynamics of life, it is creative. It's impossible for the ego to behave as if it weren't afraid of death. Fear of death can only disappear with the ego, when we take a step in mystical experience away from our ego-consciousness to the transpersonal sphere and experience there a unity that can never be doubted again. Zen tells us to die on "our cushions." Even Christian mysticism speaks about dying to the self. To the extent that our small self dies—this fearful, desperate, aggressive, opportunistic, manipulating, and seldom happy conglomerate of psychological processes—to that extent trust, joy, and hope can arise. I know many people will accuse me of not taking the ego seriously enough, which is such an essential contribution of Western culture. I have already emphasized that mystics were persons with a strong ego and that many of them were ready to be burned at the stake rather than deny their convictions. The mystic experiences "the self and more," not less of self.

Many people comfort themselves in the face of death with the hope of a continued existence in a world beyond. Or they place their hopes in reincarnation in a better earthly existence. What is the attitude of mysticism toward these ideas of resurrection and rebirth?

There's no easy answer to that question. Depending on the religious milieu of the mystic, he or she will understand those ideas in very different ways. Thus Christian mystics also speak in no uncertain terms about resurrection, although they leave open what is actually meant by the word. We humans can only imagine a continuation of life as a life of the individual self. But why shouldn't there be possibilities of existence that transcend the ego? As humans we are only one exemplar in this huge cosmos that is supposed to contain 125 billion galaxies. We suffer from an appalling egocentricity and geocentricity in assuming that this dance of the galaxies exists only for our sake. We take ourselves for the crowning achievement of the cosmos when actually we've only been creeping around as *homo sapiens* on this grain of dust for the past three million years. God, however, is timeless. He hasn't been waiting around for us for *sixteen* billion years. Resurrection is only a cipher we use for a totally different form of existence about which our reason knows nothing. On a transpersonal level, however, we sense somehow that there is a way out of the narrowness of personal existence. It is an awakening to the timelessness and spacelessness of true reality. John of the Cross called it "God awakening to himself." Our awakening is the awakening of God and our resurrection is the resurrection of God, he says.

And this awakening does not take place in mystical experience alone, but also in death?

We don't know how it is to die. But there's every reason to believe that death is an awakening. It's not a matter of a door closing, but of one opening. Whether this awakening has a personal element or not remains a moot point. God will come again in another form. Is it so important that a sort of continuity remain in existence? So-called near-death experiences suggest, at any rate, that the personality disappears and is replaced by a nonpersonal consciousness. This transformation is described in most near-death reports as fascinating and joyful, so much so that many people would rather have continued that way into death having embarked on it.

But there are also reports of near-death experiences that sound more like nightmares.

Yes, although I suspect that those negative experiences are only an intermediate stage that results when too many attachments remain in the ego-structure. The art of dying is found in letting go. Holding on results in a *horror vacui* and a horror of the "demons" we spoke about earlier.

Is that your explanation for what medieval theologians referred to as purgatory?

Indeed, it seems to me that the concept of purgatory can be useful in describing a process of detachment from the ego. Nevertheless, we would have to divest it of its negative aftertaste. This process of purification is not something negative, but a way to liberation. Thus it's important to see it as positive in spite of fear and pain, and not attempt to avoid it. The only thing that remains for us at the moment of death is letting go. Unfortunately we of the Christian world have heard too much about judgment and punishment and too little about the new dimension that lies before us. I often take walks through cemeteries. If I were a non-Christian, I would never assume that Christians believe in an afterlife. On the gravestones you see images engraved as broken pillars and broken roses. You see images of the crucified Christ, but hardly ever symbols of resurrection and a life beyond.

In Eastern religions and ways of wisdom—and incidentally also in Socrates—we encounter the idea that we have to undergo a purification or catharsis while still alive in order to more easily enter into death. Indeed, this process of purification can occur during several incarnations, according to those traditions. What relationship does this idea have to mystical spirituality?

In my opinion, genuine mysticism is not concerned about reincarnation or rebirth. Belief in rebirth belongs in the context of religion, not in the context of mysticism. Religions seek their attractiveness in the promise of salvation in a faraway future. They thus respond to the ego's need for duration. On the day of the Last Judgment, sometime in the future, everything will be put into order. One day, far in the future, evil will be punished and good will be rewarded. It makes no difference if the punishment consists in sending people to purgatory or hell or causing them to have a bad rebirth. It's also of secondary importance if the desired reward is heaven or a good rebirth. In both cases it is only our egocentricity that is served and which doesn't want to admit that the ego has to fit into the great event of the universe. Any transformation, change, or elimination of the ego seems unbearable to us.

But isn't it understandable for the ego to hope for a compensation in the next life for injustices suffered in the present life, so that the cosmic order can be achieved again?

Behind such ideas is always a petty mind that can only see God as a judge who weighs and measures things according to a merciless, mechanical law, "an eye for an eye and a tooth for a tooth." I can't help asking: Isn't such an image of God unworthy of God? Is that supposed to be the meaning of a human being and the meaning of this huge evolutionary event that we should learn moral behavior? And learn it through a primitive and merciless justice known as a "punishing God" or a "terrible rebirth"? That must be a miserable Creator indeed who makes all those who fail to make the grade repeat the school year again! No, this final judge is no bookkeeper pedantically taking notes and meting out rebirths to each person according to his or her behavior. Such an idea is much too unsatisfactory, even on an intellectual level.

But no theologian would maintain a view such as the one you just described.

To be sure, scholastic theology speaks in terms of another view of God. And scholastic theology naturally has a much more differentiated description of life in the hereafter. The situation is different in ordinary ecclesial life, however. Just take a closer look at the liturgy for burial services. It refutes all the sublime explanations of the theologians.

You said the idea of a world judgment on the last day is unsatisfactory for you. Why?

Because I consider it absurd that the human species, although it took *sixteen* billion years before we took the stage in the history of cosmic evolution, should suddenly assume the right to live on throughout eternity. That is certainly not what the process of evolution gives us to understand. What are even a hundred rebirths in comparison with the process of evolution? What are a thousand rebirths (when the average life expectancy is eighty years)? What are eighty thousand years in comparison with *fourteen* billion years, to which we could add the other hundred billion years that the cosmos was already in existence? If this single life of my existence is incapable of giving a meaning to it all, a thousand more lives won't do it either.

But don't the Eastern teachings of wisdom see things in exactly the same way? At least we can say that Buddhism teaches that, through reincarnation, the way of liberation from ego-fixation is actually only postponed to finally issue into the transpersonality of Nirvana.

In Zen Buddhism, Nirvana is not something that happens in the future. It is the naked present. Anyone who actually breaks through to this other dimension breaks through to timelessness, or we could say into the present moment. Mysticism does not speak in terms of the beyond. We have already spoken about timelessness, about the primary reality. The next world, heaven, rebirth—all of these ideas are ideally suited to founding ethics based on the pattern: If you do this or that you will have a bad rebirth. It is, however, precisely such an idea that stands in the way of genuine spiritual liberation. And then morality comes on the scene and the transpersonal sphere is effectively shut out. As a result of this moralization of religion in the hope of rebirth, our fixation on the personality increases even more and a belief in reincarnation proselytizes in favor of a perpetuation of the ego. But as long as the ego persists it will not find its meaning. We can only find meaning in it when we let go it. Our true identity lies in the divine being, which is its deepest essence. In that sense, mysticism is no less than the search for our true identity.

Please allow me a final question now at the conclusion of our discussions. You have formulated a fair number of provocative theses. We don't have to be prophets to foretell that your ideas will provoke protest and dissent. Is there anything you wish to say in reply to your critics in advance?

After what I have said, people will accuse me of not being familiar with newer currents in theology. In my bookcase you will find the catechism I studied as a child, printed in 1924, and written in the form of questions and answers. I still know a lot of the answers by heart. Next to it on the bookshelf is the *Catechism of the Catholic Church*, published in 1994, as well as a summary of Christian dogma printed in 1995 and a book on the fundamentals of theology that appeared in 2000. These books aren't just collecting dust on my bookshelves; I read and study them. And in the process I have ascertained that nothing has really changed in their basic statements. The newer interpretations might be more differentiated or subtler than the earlier ones, and this basically dualistic approach in theology remains a source of considerable difficulty for me. In so saying, I don't want to imply that I reject traditional theology. Far be it from me to do so. I simply wish to encourage discussion on these topics. The dialogue between the Eastern and Western worldview has just begun. My six years in Japan have made me realize that the Eastern approach will be a major challenge for Christians, one reason being that it is much closer to the process of evolution and the modern worldview. The twenty-first century will be a century of mysticism and metaphysics. Perhaps this book can give us a foretaste of what discussions lie before us.

Some people might ask why I have published a book of this sort in the first place. My pastoral work has shown me that the questions raised in this book urgently require answers. This book is a search for those answers. It is one attempt among many others. And that is how I would like this book to be understood. Please allow me now at the end of our discussion to quote Meister Eckhart a final time. After preaching a sermon that he was not sure people would understand, he said:

> If anyone has understood this sermon, I wish him well! If no one had come to listen, I should have had to preach it to the offering box. There are, however, certain poor people who will return home and say: "Henceforth I shall stay in my own place and eat my own bread and serve God in peace." I say, by the eternal truth, that these people will have to remain in their errors, for they will never attain what those attain who follow after God in poverty and exile! Amen."[2]

Notes

1. *Transpersonale Psychologie,* I/2000.
2. *Meister Eckhart: A Modern Translation,* by Raymond Bernard Blakney (New York: Harper and Row, 1941), 226.